Orange cat and others

~Eleven short-ish stories~

First published in Great Britain in 2020

By **Small Paper Press Ltd**.

(Independent) Southeast.

Copyright@ 2020 Anwesha Arya

Orange cat and others

Anwesha Arya

Happy Birthaday Lewis!

"We are the real countries, not the boundaries drawn on maps…" –Michael Ondaatje

The English Patient

anwesha arya

"Sometimes reality is too complex. Stories give it form."

– **Jean Luc Godard**, film director, screen writer, film critic.

STORY INDEX

Watching Ants

It's way past sleep now. I watch a crack in the wall.

Suddenly I see two tiny specs moving steadily closer.

Ants.

They glide perfectly in a soundless world, trailing closer to a point beside the crack, where they stop and confer. For a breathless instant I wonder if one of them will alter its course to join the other. A tap drips, laughing too loudly in the kitchen. They back away from each other a second, disturbed or maybe listening. Then they continue on their separate ways. I don't wonder where they're going. I still watch the white space between them.

It grows greater and greater.

Then, I can no longer watch them both at once. I have to follow one or the other with my eyes, but which? Before I decide they're both out of sight, and it's just the blank wall with me staring. I'm bored, I've lost them now, but ants never did satisfy my appetite. I settle for fleas in my paws instead.

Black Pearl

Leena had her day off every Sunday. There was no one else at home. Mukta liked being alone. Then she heard someone, or something, move in their old box room. She listened outside the shut door. Silence. She opened the door slowly, a sweet smell poured out. It was the silent hay lining the box that had held *hapoos* mangoes. It smelled like wet toffee in your mouth, only warmer and darker. Then she saw the small shuffling kittens pushing a box of empty bottles. Mukta relaxed.

The mother cat woke and stretched slender hairy paws onto the black mattress she was curled on. Her mouth ugly, in a lip-stretching yawn, wider than wide. As she stretched an old bottle-opener jumped off the bumpy mattress onto the floor, beside the door. The clink of metal on tile woke four kittens, and they began to mew at their pink-marmalade mother.

Just below it the empty crate was breathing now, with a fresh mango scent.

'They're hungry', thought Mukta shutting the door behind her. The kittens were still tiny, their eyes not yet pricked but their folded ears heard everything. They'd be blind for another week yet, listening made them learn. Mukta wanted some bubble-wrap to make the cover for her unwritten Chemistry project. Bubble-wrap would be perfect to represent atoms, with its many globes of tight packed air that farted when you punched them between your thumbnails, just like Janvi, her cousin, who loved eating *phoolgobi parathas*. Janvi loved stuffed cauliflower *parathas*, which made you horribly gassy, everyone knew that. Mukta had been collecting cut-up issues of *National Geographic* and *Span* in a big card box.

Where was that grey box now?

Her project was due in a week and she hadn't even begun reading up. She'd been too busy with podgy Putchkin, helping her to birth the kittens and then keep them here in hiding. Three kittens were paler shades of their mother's marmalade coat, one was bright black. They all had pink triangles for noses. Mukta snuggled into their wet baby breath, smelling of sugary milk, thick and warm. Baba would be mad if he knew she was keeping them at all. He hated cats; they're not loyal like dogs are, he said.

Putchkin was her mother's cat.

The kittens took up most of Mukta's time after school. This week they'd gotten hungrier, so she hadn't had a moment to even think about atoms, let alone molecular theory. It was tough enough being in the Ninth Standard with all the assignments and her new class Prefect's post. But she also had to manage the house, keeping a check on smooth-eyed Leena's dusting. Then there was her slow sad father.

Mukta knelt on the mattress. Cotton bulged, plopping in a puddle of ooze all over the floor. She stroked the tiniest black kitten above its wet nose. The sturdiest kitten kept pulling at its, Putchkin's, thinned tail. It reminded her of Samit.

He had won a scholarship to Oxford University, without even studying for it.

Her elder brother worked part-time at a bank in London where he was studying. Samit was brilliant, like Baba who was a physics professor at one of the best colleges in Bombay and a visiting scholar at BARC. She hated that name. It held the sound of all their arguments, like water frozen in broken freezer. Her parents had flung cold water in their words every night, drenching each other with them, before they finally separated. Rather, before Maa left. Though Mukta was now sixteen she had never really got on with her mother. She loved her, yes.

But that was all.

Mukta had really curly elbow length hair, not quite black, but touched with sunlit brown. Along with her grim glasses a pressed frown perched above her nose. Mukta had worn since the day her mother left. Mukta or 'Pearl', as her catholic boyfriend insisted on calling her, was quite talkative on the outside, but in her head the silence was deafening.

***

A door slammed shut beyond the box-room echoing down the corridor. Baba was back from Anjana auntie's house. It was nearing lunchtime. Mukta suddenly wished they had never left Calcutta where Baba's cousin Jhumpa *pishi* lived. They had tried to settle down there. So far west of Bombay Mukta knew the train journey lasted more than two days, but flight had felt longer than the two and a half hours. Baba wanted to leave her there, under 'female' care. That had been three months ago, Mukta was so close to her sixteenth birthday, that he felt it she would need a woman around. But Mukta remained stubborn and silent, 'Bombay, is *home* Baba'. Now, after seeing Calcutta she missed the tram rides, the slowness of the streets, and the lazing sunbeams on the lake. Those were strange lumpy old streets opening onto broader roads where slug-like trams left silver trails embedded in a tarred road.

Mukta heard her father's approaching footsteps and hurried to her feet. She snapped her mind shut of trams tugging silver across roads in Calcutta and stood straight. Then she rummaged behind her under the wooden bench and pulled a cardboard box forward. It jangled with un-used Christmas decorations. She bundled the three kittens into their kitchen duster and laid them back inside, leaving the box open. Where was the little black one? Maybe it had crawled behind the boxes. It really was dim in here, and the mattress too was black. Oh, there it was, but the door had opened.

Baba stood silently, the blue poured from under his arms more like water than light. The box room still smelled faintly sweet, like the chocolate icing on her last birthday cake. That's what it reminded her of that first cake only she and Baba had cut. It would be the fourth birthday since Maa had left. That first had been just her and Baba.

'Mukta? Are you in here? What's that smell…toffee?' He sniffed the dim air, taking a step into the room. Something clanked, skipping across the floor; he looked at the odd piece of metal at his feet.

'Ah, there you are, not crying are you?' Her father in his grey Sunday T-shirt bent down peering at her.

'Why would I be…?' Mukta tried not to sound irritated.

'Oh! I thought … Janvi is on the phone. Mithali and all of them are going to Kanheri Caves for a picnic, they want you to...'

'No, Baba I *can't* go, I've got this project to complete...could you tell her please...I'll...?'

He relaxed his frown but looked confused, '...don't you even want to talk to her?'

'I'll call her back later...I'm sorry Baba, could you, please? Thanks. I have to find this kit...chen paper thing, I mean box...'

'Right.'

He still looked confused, but left. Baba was really short-sighted without his glasses; he often forgot he wasn't even wearing them. It was not surprising that he rarely saw things right in front of him.

'I'll tell her,' he said as he shut the door.

Once she was sure he was out of earshot she picked out the kittens one by one. One was chewing a holly leaf; obviously mistaking the thick felt for its warm mother. She laid them back onto the mattress. The black one had tangled itself in some yellow satin beside the door, right behind where her father had been standing. Thank goodness he hadn't seen it, so brightly wrapped, a little wobbly package. She picked it free, giggling nervously and laid it down beside the others who were now bumbling clumsily across the mattress like beads from a broken necklace.

'Uuuf! Shush, just stay on the duster please…no, no don't eat the cotton, you'll sneeze you silly meow!'

Behind the box of Christmas bits she finally found the other box she had come searching for. Under the magazines were some sheets of un-punctured bubble-wrap; it would do fine. She pulled free a half cut sheet of red crepe, and coughed over a pile of grimy magazines. This was it; old copies of *Scientific American* and *Span* lay under slashed issues of *National Geographic*.

Great, some research material was bound to be in there. Ah, here was a cover story on 'Chemical Compositions of the Electron'. Lucky me, she thought, I'll be done by this coming weekend for sure. She wiped her fingers on her denim cut-offs and tickled Whiskers' now flattish tummy. The kittens were feeding. She watched them for a moment, then turned and left.

'Mukta', her father called as she walked out pulling the box-room door shut. 'Do you want some baked beans on toast? Hm?'

Baked beans, it was his Sunday brunch usual. On Leena's days off and on Sundays Baba loved pretending he was back in his 'bachelor pad', as he called it, in London. He'd begun talking a lot about that period of his life now. It was before he had met her mother, Heera.

Heera. Short, ravishing and unfriendly. They were so unalike, Baba and Heera. Mukta was very different from Heera as well. She had darker heavy hair, not delicate brush strokes like Heera had. Mukta was tall, like her father, so she didn't ever want to wear heels. But Heera, always the diamond, glittered in expensive stilettos studded with bits of glass and gold. Mukta hated gold, she was allergic to its warm touch, she could wear only silver. Heera wore dainty curls of gold in almost every orifice of her sculpted body. Across her magenta-edged fingers and in her small round ears, even her sharp edged nose had a fine stud that glinted when she was angry.

Mukta, never quite saw her mother, she saw expensive looking clothes, shrouded in strong fragrances. She could identify those smells anywhere, thinking that's Maa's black scent, and that's her purple one. But she had stopped calling her Maa a month before she left. She had seen Baba curdling hard into himself, his eyes growing passive and horrible. She blamed Heera for it.

After Samit left five years ago she'd hardly stayed here with them. She would go over to her mother's place at Nepean Sea Road, 'Mukta you can come stay the night if you like?' But I don't like, Mukta used to think. Then Heera had begun traveling a lot, especially to England. Baba would slouch harder and speak less, like he had a perpetual tummy-ache. Then Heera began to visit Samit in London, sometimes four months at a time, sometimes longer. Why didn't she just leave forever? Mukta had wished.

If she never comes back I'll look after him, Mukta thought on her eleventh birthday. Baba bought a Pillsbury cake mix from the grocer with green eyes who sold other smuggled things like Tang and Mentos, crowded on dark white shelves. Baba baked her cake the night before, just for the two of them. He even got her blue magic candles. She loved how they refused to blow out. How much she had laughed. They had laughed together. Heera never baked for her, only for Samit, her Sam. He was his mother's little prince. He should've been spoiled but he was quite a good elder brother. Samit was caring and always helped her especially with literature, which Mukta hated mugging up. He made her understand language and taught her Shylock's speech from *The Merchant of Venice*. He explained where to stress and sigh, and how to breathe right. He was an effortless teacher and actor. Exactly like their mother, very unlike her. She missed him now; though she hated admitting it she was jealous of how much Maa adored him. It was obvious why; Mukta wasn't an inch like her mother, Sam with his light curling hair was.

Then suddenly one Sunday she had really gone. That had been the thirteenth of August, just after she had entered the Fifth Standard and senior school.

Her father's soft voice grabbed her back to the present from inside her head.
'Baked beans are good for you, though bacon's not!' She walked into their large green and yellow tiled kitchen lined with clear glass cabinets. It always looked spotless, like in Heera's Ikea catalogues, as if no one cooked there. Just as matched in those World of Interiors magazines.

'Where's the damned tin-opener...this Leena...'

'Here', she said shutting the cutlery drawer behind her.

'I love cooking on Sunday afternoon, so peaceful, nah?'

Yup, sweet Baba, boiling eggs in a precise pan of water, just four and a half minutes, heating red beans from a can with an inch of coriander. True cooking!

'Shall I cut you some onions?'

He stopped, 'So you *have* been crying, haven't you?'

'No, Baba. *Why?*' she couldn't help the creeping irritation in her voice.

'You've just been so off lately, these past two weeks at least. I do notice these things you know. I hardly see you after school you disappear, and then at the dinner table you're so quiet.' So, he had noticed. 'And you spend too much time in that airless store room.'

Her father turned and looked directly at her 'I should have sent you with Mithali just now, shouldn't I? She's so good at this stuff.' Mithali was his brother's wife. Mukta tried to outstare his gaze. He finally relented.

'But I'm glad you didn't go. I...I didn't want to eat alone.' He looked pale in the sunlight; they hadn't been to Marve beach for many weekends now like they used to. He never went to Goa anymore. Earlier, they would drive down whenever it was okay to miss a few days of school.

He turned back to the bubbling pan. Almost ceremonially he dropped fine bits of green over the bubbling beans.

'So, who's Robin?' His grey back stared at her, creaseless in the afternoon sun. It was slanting fiercely through the open window. The air smelled of salt and eruptions of coriander.

'He's my boyfriend, he's also Jenny auntie's son', she replied, almost too casually. He'd never asked before.

'Jenny? Who *is* Jenny auntie?' He was stirring the beans as they bubbled more furiously. Mukta walked up to the gas range and turned the flame down to simmer. 'Hmmm,' he murmured in thanks.

'She used to swim with, with Mm…'

It fell spread-eagled, an awkward blotch on the sunny floor.

'Aha!' he said in recognition turning to her, '*Jenny*. Ah Raunit and Jenny…'

Then he saw her face.

Mukta was looking positively blanched; she could feel her skin stretched thin with sweat, and she was breathing funny. Almost not at all. Her eyes behind the weightless frames must have looked too wide to be held in her face. Her fists were ready to punch the air, clutched and white. 'Why was I named Mukta, Dad?'

She only called him 'Dad' when she was asking something crucial, it was never planned, it just happened. He smiled an even sort of smile, like a clean slab of butter when you've smeared it and can't wipe the traces clean. Guilty.

'Did *she* name me?'

'No! I did', he said vehemently, suddenly like ice, he looked at the bloodless edge of his toenail.

'Why? Because it **went** with her name?'

'Huh? Oh, I see you mean like diamond and pearl...no damn it, it was because I was trying so hard, I was fighting really hard to...to... I wanted a daughter I wanted you. Do you know how a pearl is made?'

It was quiet in the kitchen, inside her head it felt like being behind a windscreen in the rain.

'Yes,' she said, feeling the spark of a tear on her left cheek. She straightened her back, she wouldn't cry in front of him. 'It's very painful for the oyster; it's a fleck of sand isn't it? A small bit of sand or something gets trapped in its soft flesh and the oyster gets hurt and irritated and coats it in these solutions it secretes, some chemical secretions, something to make it feel softer to the sensitive flesh, and that forms a pearl right?'

'It's a painful process, yes.'

'Does the oyster die?'

'No it loses part of itself to create something beautiful and magical.'

Mukta still felt like she was watching slow silent rain on curved glass.

'Dad,' her voice grated with trying, '*why did she go? I'm old enough now. You said you'd tell me when I was old enough.'

He looked like something vital had drained from his eyes. Baba was getting older, and sadder. She longed to shout out loud. But I'm here Baba, and I'm not going anywhere can't you see?

He turned the flame off, and pulled two slices of thick brown bread from the oven, where they'd been toasting. He wrapped them in an ochre napkin, and said 'I'm glad you like yellow.' Mukta had recently bought yellow napkins to replace the old green ones.

'BABA! You're changing the subject?' she raised her voice, and then smiled, 'of course I like yellow, you know I'm like you that way!'

'Are you, really?'

'Daaad!'

'I don't know Mukta. I don't know why she left. Maybe I didn't understand who she was. She said…she wanted…are you old enough?' He looked at her; she noticed how his eyes looked lighter than they were sometimes. Like honey under sunlight.

'I've had a boyfriend for a year; I've had my periods for three. I know you don't get pregnant by French kissing in the garage…'

'You did what…?'

'It's just a way of saying it…but seriously Dad, tell me…'

Mukta watched her father's face, her fingers tensing. 'She wanted something different. That's what she said. I don't play cards, I don't like smoking, and I hate club talk. She grew up there. Sitting on the balcony of Bombay Gymkhana sipping daiquiris on ice…'

'But you did too? Didn't you? I mean Dadu was a member, isn't that where you two met?'

'No.'

She looked at him as he swallowed half a chunk of toast dripping red sauce.

'No, we didn't meet there', he continued, when he was almost through chewing. 'Your Dadu, my Baba, was a member being a famous gynaecologist and all –but our circles were entirely different.'

'But didn't you fall in love?'

He smiled that wiped butter smile again. 'I don't think so.'

'Then how…I mean, I always thought…'

He was staring at his empty plate. Traces of sauce spread fingers of tomato colouring across its white surface. He looked at it intently, as if that colour was the most important thing he had seen in a long time.

'My father met her father in the Cigar Room at the Gymkhana. They became friends. Heera was studying Literature like everyone else at the time, at St. Catherine's in Oxford. I was in London at Kings College; I hadn't made it to the Oxbridge set. Apparently she got involved with her tutor there; she was just twenty. When she came home for the holidays for the second time, her mother discovered that she was three months or so…'

'Sam…Samit? Dad, he's not my our I mean your…' The rain inside her head was steady and pouring.

He smiled at her sudden alert sharpness, as if his favourite perfume bottle had pierced him, breaking as his hand closed around it.

'No, he's not, but…'

'BUT...? I've always been so jealous of him and he's doing medicine at the London School of Hygiene, I thought he inherited all your brains...and he's got the bank job this summer and he's got...'

'...He's got grey eyes, and you've got your mother's eyes' He smiled, and Mukta ignored his last observation. She didn't want to remember.

'But Baba I don't get it...what exactly...'

'Well, she apparently wanted to go back, but her parents were too shocked ashamed even. She wasn't showing yet. They were furious, at least her father was. She called Oxford to tell him, the tutor I mean, but apparently his wife answered the phone. So Heera never went back. I had just returned home to Bombay after completing my doctorate. London had been very uneventful for me. A few sweet, not so serious, girlfriends because I knew Maa would find me someone. I had no idea.'

'How could they expect you to...to I mean? You accepted?!'

'Apparently there was some complication with her situation medically as well. They couldn't ab... you know get rid...without endangering her life in the bargain.'

'She was already in her fourth month you said...' Mukta's voice was steady.

'You have grown up haven't you?'

'... Daaad, what happened then?'

Her face was bright with anxiety for the young man in the story who was her father. He sat, his fingers entwined his chin resting on them, staring at the light above her head outside the window. Her curly hair, the same shade as the fuzz on his arms and head, shone in a halo round her wider eyes.

'Well, by this time Heera's father and my Baba had known each other almost five or six years. They only met at the Gymkhana though. Their situations in life were so different. Heera's father owned things. A stallion and three mares, they managed two petrol pumps in the city. For him gold cuff links were a matter of course. My father had bought his way into that world because of his deft hands and medical acumen. He always wore a dark grey safari suit, buttoned to the chin. Those suits were so well starched they scraped his smooth chin.' He looked down at his hands remembering, and then added, 'They didn't really 'fit' as friends, I guess.'

'But what happened...'

'Heera was formally introduced to me. My father explained the situation to me on our way to their house.' He took a slow breath. Mukta felt like he was leaving something out, but she didn't want to break his flow with questions. 'Their house was palatial. She looked so vulnerable surrounded by all those tall vases and statues. She looked so small. Frankly I felt brave and very, what's the word…protective I guess, like I was rescuing this poor young girl. She was really ravishing, and hardly showing at that stage…I think she found me attractive, I remember her holding my hand really tight when her parents left the room. I was twenty-six; she looked so good, really good. She seemed petite and sweet…' He looked almost young as he unclasped his long thick fingers and touched his eyebrow.

'Yes I know she did,' Mukta had seen their wedding pictures, fading behind the hankies on her father's shirt shelf, and marvelled at how little Heera had aged.

'I believed Baba knew what was best. We met only a couple of times before the day of the registry.' Her father sighed with his shoulders; a slight wheeze escaped his lips. The sun was on his face but suddenly his eyes didn't shine at all.

'The story they circulated was that we'd met in England and fallen in love'.

He paused, a half smile between his cheek and lip.

'She was kept almost under surveillance at her home. Even I didn't visit her much. The few times we met she'd just look at me and hold my hand tight again. She mostly talked about Oxford, how much she adored it. She asked me if I'd enjoyed London. That's what we seemed to have in common. It was also rumoured that we'd already got married abroad, with consent. And that now we'd have a small exclusive reception.'

He swallowed some air. 'I hardly remember it. I didn't know more than five people. Heera looked healthy suddenly and quite stunning. She smiled a lot but didn't say a word. She kept squeezing my hand, as though I was her fellow conspirator. I believed it for some time myself. We moved into this flat that her father bought for us.' He took a deep breath from the mug of coffee. He gulped it down; she heard the sound of wetness falling down his throat.

'I'd rather have stayed with Maa and Baba, but Akhilesh and Mithali were in the second bedroom and Gamdevi isn't exactly Malabar Hill. Also Mithali was expecting Ajay then. Baba seemed very pleased at the reception. I didn't really notice till I saw the photos later. He had been positively grinning at the party, and he looked even fatter, both truly uncharacteristic. Then I realised their relationship was finally equal, in the Cigar Room and outside.'

Mukta suddenly felt like an eavesdropper who has crept in on a conversation that reveals something scandalous about the person you love most.

'Heera didn't really stay with me that first year. She had Samit at her mother's place. I concentrated on either returning to London on a Research fellowship or finding a suitable job. He was a beautiful baby. When he opened his transparent grey eyes and looked at me I realised, probably for the first time, that he wasn't mine.'

Mukta shifted her bare feet, itching the arch of her left foot with her right toe. 'That's when I decided I wanted a daughter; it came like the bang of warm blood into my head.' He smiled down at his hands, she couldn't make out whether he looked sad or not. Then he looked up, but past her face again.

'Samit spent a lot of time with her parents. I guess they were giving us time to really get to know each other. I realised then how Heera's devotion to her tutor had led very quickly to love, then just as sharply to hate and anger. I began to see who she was. I became so lonely Mukta*baba*, really lonely.'

Mukta listened; the rain in her head slowing to a drizzle.

'I was still trying to get funding when, at the end of two years in Bombay, Maa contracted Hepatitis. She became very weak. I postponed my fellowship plan. Baba needed me. I'll never forget how Heera looked that afternoon.'

'I came home from the hospital and told her I had decided against going back to England. It was like I'd slapped her. She stopped talking to me. Samit and I got on fine though. He was a gentle, intelligent child. Even he couldn't understand the way she fretted and fussed but never said a thing. He would just climb into my lap when she ignored him. Finally when I took up the teaching position she left to stay with her mother again. It would last a few months I thought. Then she had Samit picked up one weekend couple of weeks after she had left.'

'I guess she was counting on returning to the UK for a while. My Maa died suddenly after a tortured three months. Samit was enrolled at Bombay International, your mother's school. Things were difficult; they started staying at Nepean Sea Road permanently. I rarely saw her, but she kept up appearances well. She didn't even look like a mother. Her figure was trimmer than before she'd had Samit.'

'She came back here when I was
promoted to Head of Department and the
Bhabha Centre offered me the scholarship. There
was a chance I would have to travel between
London and here. It felt good to have their
voices in these rooms again. That's when I
decided I wanted you really badly. One day, a
few months after she returned I spoke to Heera.
She refused, she didn't want all that pain again
she said. She was on the pill, I'm sure
you...hmm, so I decided to wait a couple of
years more. I got two letters from London in the
meantime they were looking for resident
Physicists. Heera urged me to accept the offer,
but I needed to stay and develop work here. I
was happier here, at home. When Samit was five
I reminded Heera, I had also spoken to her
mother. She knew the reality of our relationship.
She agreed that the best thing would be for us to
have a child of our own. I filled Samit's head
with the idea of a younger sibling, someone to

look after, to play with.'

'Heera for all her lack of maternal instinct was crazy about Sam, as she called him. She began to avoid me. I became almost frantic. She shifted into the guestroom; I used it as a study then, and it couldn't be locked from the inside there was no bolt then. I began keeping an eye on her diary, checking the circled dates. Then one afternoon, it was a bank holiday; I came back from the college library early. She had just come back from her swim and was napping.' He fell silent and began staring at the unpolished table.

***

Sumontro could see her clearly as if she was lying there in front of him, just a touch away. He felt he could smell the musky odour that clung around her lithe body after a shower. She always had a hot shower no matter what month of the year it was, it made her skin cooler to touch and so supple. He watched her breathing asleep for more than twenty minutes. He saw the swell of her hips like a river under monsoon, longing to touch the tips of exposed skin where her nightshirt had fallen open. He sucked on his tongue tasting the coffee but remembering another more distinctive taste not unlike overripe raspberries. He clasped his fingers remembering her face when she turned sensing him in the room and saw his eyes above her belly. He had held her like men are told to grip unwilling wives. Her waist had felt so small; he hadn't touched her in years. She was firm from months of swimming, her thighs refused to part until his bare knee wedged itself into her space. She hadn't squirmed, just stared at him with a clear cold glare. He had enjoyed the power of her tiny hands

under his chest, he hadn't even taken his shirt off, and
her satin negligee had peeled off her breasts like the
skin of a ripe mango. He sucked her fragrance and
held back his pleasure in his thickening throat. Her
eyes hadn't shut once; she had glared at him, wide
and absolutely silent until her mouth had finally
opened in that unconscious physical submission. He
had continued to hold her under him, hoping she
would sense the comfort of his caress. She hadn't.

***

Mukta stared at her father with her mother's eyes. His silence was a lot louder than the night inside her *razai*, lying awake under the cotton spread afraid of the dark, missing a mother who read aloud only to her son. He wasn't looking at anything. She didn't dare speak.

She suddenly realised it wasn't the reflected red from Baba's enamel coffee mug, but real blood flushed in his face. He closed his eyes then opened them.

'That was the thirteenth of August. It poured like mad for three days after that, we stayed in the guestroom. She refused to talk to me, but I didn't let that matter.'

He went silent again, remembering. Heera had smelled so good, like orchids would smell if they had conceded to having a perfume. Anjana used the same perfume, but on her it smelled like wet mud and new flowers. Anjana was taller, sturdier, he had never liked small women, but Heera was exquisite, he remembered how the cup of his hand concealed the swell of her breast. He looked at his empty hands, speaking slowly.

'Samit spent that long weekend at Mithali's house; he and Ajay were inseparable. Heera's parents were away in Delhi. With her mother away and Samit back in the house she couldn't run away. I had spoken to her gynaecologist, remember Raman uncle? He was Baba's student. I asked him to tell me if she went for any appointment I hadn't fixed for her. When her mother came back and heard the news she was excited for us. I knew it wouldn't work the way she wished, but I didn't care anymore. I got what I wanted…I knew it was over. Her stare…'

Mukta wanted to ask a lot of things, but they stuck like candy in a cavity. Let him talk, just let him talk.

He continued speaking in a slow deliberate tone.

'Heera and I had never been more distant. She hardly *spoke* to me anyway. She got a Yale lock fixed on the guestroom door. She threw all my books out. I began working in our bedroom. At the end of the day we'd dissolve into our separate spaces.'

Dissolve? She remembered the hard slam of her mother's room door like a jam bottle breaking. Only there was no gooey stuff spilt anywhere, just a deep inside sticky feeling with bits of glass poking out.

'She clammed up. I was to blame too. I never did anything. If I bought flowers I never bought orchids, I'd just leave them on the kitchen table for Leena to arrange. I never gave her anything. I didn't think I could.'

He got up and cleared their plates. She didn't interrupt his Sunday routine of washing up; he enjoyed it. She thought it was weird, but then enjoying washing once a week was okay maybe. She was thinking too hard; her thoughts pushed against the inside of her head, dripping a question or two. But she couldn't ask anything. The afternoon grew softer on the yellow floor, while she listened to the plash of water against the steel basin.

'Do you want something more?' he asked, not looking at her.

'There's some cake and ice cream in the fridge, I'll get it.' She tied the yellow napkin into knots like her throat. He seemed stuck to the tap.

'I can't believe that was really fifteen years ago. I really wanted a daughter. I have never wanted, really wanted anything from her, even from life. She accused me once of having no ambition. She was right maybe...I never resented Samit, though her bond with him is incredible. I love that boy. I got a letter from him the other day. Heera was with him two months ago. He's doing well. He says Heera is buying a house in Oxford, she's working on some medieval literature project with some Samuel Beckman at her old university.'

He played with the kitchen towel, wiping each plate twice then slipping them into the slats of the draining rack. He stood suddenly very straight, as if something heavy had just slipped from his shoulders onto the floor.

Mukta thought she heard a shattering in the distance. The rain inside her head stopped and she looked at the sunlight outside the window growing peachier.

'So. You know now, you *are* old enough aren't you?'

He was actually grinning; the grey T-shirt looked dull below his face.

'I am, huh?' she heard herself say, and then grinned too.

He went over to the fridge.

'Beer?' he said, looking over at her, across the bright floor. Mukta felt like he'd just opened the door to his world. The cool waft of ice and beer and chocolate cake brushed past into her hair.

'Ya! Let's have a beer Dad!'

She grinned.

His expression was hilarious. His eyebrows danced up into his hair then dropped like a deflated balloon. But his face had filled with sunshine.

'Uh. So. Have you heard of Shandy? Here, there's some 7-up, that's nicer than just beer by itself? Can be bitter the first time.' He warned.

She couldn't help laughing. Suddenly everything seemed fine. He was opening and shutting all the drawers, 'Where's the opener? Have you seen it? Really! I never understand Leena's logic...how she organizes...no it isn't here.'

He stopped.

'Wait, didn't I just see it...'

He shut the last drawer and left the room. Mukta was holding the gold bottle of murmuring beer to her hot temple. Where's he off to, she wondered. Then she remembered: the old opener lying on the box-room floor! Oh hell the kittens! She put the bottle down.

Her father stood in the doorway, the bottle opener in his mouth and the tiny black kitten, still swathed in yellow satin, curled in his bent elbow. He was actually stroking it.

'So this is who's been taking up all your evenings huh?'

Mukta sort of smiled. 'So young woman, what shall we call it?'

'Pearl' she said, quietly.

Sturdy Paper Boats

On her birthday Reena wrote in her diary:

Monday, 13th June

6.23 am

I am thirteen today.

I got up at 6.05. No actually it was just six. I wanted to see my face in the mirror when I turned from twelve to thirteen. I was born at 6.05 but I set the alarm for six because I wasn't sure if I should wash my face before looking at myself! But I did. I had to, there was white stuff in my eyes, I couldn't see me clearly enough! I kept thinking something wild and crazy will happen. But nothing happened…I just dropped the pencil cup off the desk…I hope Didun didn't hear it.

I don't think she did…she usually sleeps deepest just before she wakes up at 6.45 sharp; every day for forty years she says. That's calculating since when she married Dadu. I wonder if I could do that, wake up bang at the same time every day without an alarm clock. No one else is up yet; the house is really mousy (is that right? Have to check the dictionary, my new one).

Actually, at my party yesterday, Sonali told us that her sister believed if you wish for something on your birthday, at exactly the time when you were born, you get it. She and Sonali both did, and their wishes came true. So I wanted to try. But I can't say what I wished for, that's against the wishing rule. If you tell your wish won't happen!

My face isn't different but my eyes look brighter, but that could be coz it rained the whole night...the sky was so so red in the evening, like Montuda's face when Meena Mami's catches him smoking in the bathroom!!! Only a much nicer red and the smells are definitely better than that horrid smoke he leaves behind. It's so bugging his school bus comes ten minutes before mine so I always have to have a bath after him...it's truly horrid. I love that word...horrid, it really sounds like what it means, I got it out of Enid Blyton when I was ten and have used it religiously since. I was really looking forward to thirteen. It's a really big number, so much more grown up than twelve. I always want to be thirteen. I'm also really excited because school's re-opening today; it's a Monday. That's why we had my birthday party yesterday...I was so happy when it poured all evening. Tina, Sonia, Preeti and Rohit and Raghu, and even Sonali thought it was a 'drag', they wanted to play hide-and-seek in the garden. Didun's garden is so huge and full of tall bushy plants. But I play

*there every evening. I wanted to play sensible games
like passing the parcel and treasure hunt. I mean it
was a birthday party not just a tea party or
something. I made all the treasure hunt clues into
rhyming couplets without Meena Mami's help. It was
really a proper treasure hunt, not like just shouting
'hot' or 'warm' or 'cold'. I think it was brilliant. I had
sooper fun.*

*After they all went I just wanted to sit and
watch the rain from Mamu's room. It's the first room
to get the rain in, but Didun wouldn't let me sit till I
changed. She made me change out of my yellow lace
frock; it was itching my chin and my back anyway. I
hate party clothes; my torn jeans are 'coolest', like
Raghu says. She actually didn't want me to sit
watching the rain anyway; she always thinks I'll get a
cold. I tried to explain to her last year that the rain
loves me. It'll never make me sick. Nothing you truly
love can ever make you sick, nah? At least I think so.*

Anyway, I'm dying to go to school. My bag is all packed with new, clean books. I love the way they smell when you open them for the first time. Fresh crisp pages and a blue pencil box from Didun full of new tall-sharpened pencils. It's yummy really. Mamu thinks I'm an idiot for loving school, especially the first day. But I think he's an idiot, how can it not be exciting when there's a whole new year waiting for you. And new things to learn from new teachers, and new leaves on the trees because of the rain...and new friends to make. How can I make him see he's always so bored? He really bugs me.

Maybe I'll find my special best friend this year, that someone I can tell EVERYTHING to. Anyway, I'm looking new, I grew my hair in the holidays and these awful braces will come off in a month's time. I'm going to make a bouncy ponytail for school; it's so thick and wavy just like Maa's. I miss her. But I love it here at Didun's place, she spoils me and I adore her. I'm not wearing my party dress to school…I'm wearing my crispy new uniform and I've grown two inches!! I'm really thirteen and the world outside smells divine.

PS: Ma said she'd call tonight. She sent me a card that sings in three languages French and English and one confusing one…I opened it just now, Didun wouldn't let me see it yesterday even after the party. It came on Friday. Ma remembers everything. I love Ma. There, Didun's given that big gruntyy snore; she'll be up any minute. Better get ready!

Reena wrote in her diary every day, sometimes twice a day. It was her own voice speaking to herself. It got lonely in her grandmother's house. Her mother, Nayonika had left her there for the past year now. Reena's parents were going through an ugly spilt-up, so her mother thought it would be better for Reena to spend the last crucial years of school under the guardianship of her grandmother. Shomu, her father wasn't very pleased with the idea, but he didn't have a better alternative.

That's how Reena came to live in the sprawling bungalow at Mount Mary Road. She walked down the twin Mount Mary steps every day to the bottom of the hill, to get the school bus and up again in the evenings when she came home. She was a sunny girl, tall for her age with a lion's mane of hair on her head. She was slow at school though, the only outward sign of a broken home. She was popular; always the joker, but she hadn't found that special friend.

For the past year her loneliness had grown. This maturity pushed onto her was becoming something of a burden. She tried to concentrate at school, and only half succeeded but somehow coming home was the problem. She needed to find a way out of her thoughts. Reena couldn't understand why her grandmother reminded her three times a day, 'Don't frown Reena…do you want lines like mine? So young…' On her last summer holiday with her mother she realised she must stop her automatic frown. She must always look happy, if she didn't Ma felt pressured and began blaming herself.

'Why did I marry him? It's just made a mess for you. It's not your fault, this has nothing to do with you and now you won't have a father. It's my stupidity, I feel so guilty. Shomu is *so* charming, he promised so much. I'm sorry Ree, so sorry.'

'Sometimes', Reena thought, 'Ma forgets how old I am'.

At other times these confessions made her feel responsible and even proud. But she was tired; tired of watching her mother cry, tired of feeling the anger and helplessness of being unable to console her properly. She began to feel like she was the burden on her mother. She laughed on the outside, and kept a little lockable diary inside, hidden in the underwear drawer of Meena Mami's cupboard, which she now used.

Over the last year at Didun's her only real
enemy had been Montuda, her elder cousin, who
was a younger version of Mamu. He bullied her
just to watch her run. He called her names like
'dragon-teeth' and 'Edwina-scissor-fangs'. How
she wished they'd send him away to a boarding
school for retarded boys. He regularly nicked
cigarettes from their driver Arjunda and read
dirty magazines. This treasure he kept well
hidden, wrapped in a dark plastic bag taped to
the inside of the flush cabinet. The first Sunday,
soon after she moved in with them she
discovered his stash. He was doing something
disgusting with his fist in his lap when she
walked into the bathroom to fill a vase for some
garden flowers. She wanted to cheer-up the
room she was sharing with Didun. No one else
was home. Didun was taking a snore-filled nap.
He had obviously forgotten to lock the door. She
saw him; pants down a look of pained happiness
on his bloated red face and the flush cabinet

gaping open. She rushed out. Then made a dash to hide somewhere in the garden, giggling hard inside her throat, but scared.

He came and found her some fifteen minutes later, up in the *Champa* tree, now her favourite hiding place. He asked her to come down from that frangipani tree.

'Look, Reenu', ugh she hated his slimy tone. She hated it more when he pretended to blend affection into his raspy voice, calling her 'Reenu'. She hated him, his red face and his big body. 'Look', he repeated, trying to get her attention. She couldn't bear to 'look' especially at his hands. He stared up at her into the tree without speaking, she was glad she had changed out of her school skirt and was wearing her sturdy jeans. She heard him mumble so looked down, mocking deep concentration, as if she was praying.

'I'm sorry I forgot to shut the door.'

He paused, breathing heavily. She felt like he expected her to say something, but her lips felt glued. She knew if she dared open her mouth she would either guffaw or puke right onto him. Montu's garbled words filtered through the leaves to her silent ears. 'I don't know if you understand any of this stuff yet...but it's something boys have to do. It makes us men, *see*.'

'I certainly don't *want* to *see*', she thought.

But she nodded a little too vigorously pretending to be very understanding of this terrible ailment of being a man. As she nodded her head the flowers shook droplets of dew onto her ears, tickling her. She wished she could climb up higher. She just wanted him to go away. Reena looked at him finally; she thought he looked like a peculiarly ugly pig.

'Don't worry, I won't tell on you', she said aloud. And yet she didn't want to let him get away so lightly, not after all those times he had bullied her.

'But now …you owe me one…' her voice trailed off, the unspoken threat hung like a daring drop of dew on a green leaf tip.

The scent of freshly wet *Champa* blooms filled her head, these fragrant frangipani flowers had always brought memory flooding back. This was how a cornered animal felt, Reena thought; hiding up in a tree waiting for its stalker to tire of waiting. Montu looked peculiar, calculating something under his eyebrows, which knotted themselves like hairy caterpillars mating. Then he slowly grinned, his maroon lips swinging out of shape. Reena couldn't tell what was worse, his smile or his frown.

'I'll let you ride my cycle every Saturday and I'll go to Divesh's house whenever I like. That way he won't come over here, and you can tell Ma and Didun I'm studying with your friend Sonali's elder brother's help whenever I go there straight after school' Reena flinched. If Montuda was bad, Divesh was seriously retarded. He was the supplier of the brown-paper wrapped magazines parading as Geography workbooks, which they pored over in Montu's study room that Reena had to share with them while doing her homework. Reena got a creepy feeling every time Divesh came over to apparently study; though he never spoke to her or even stared. It was the way he licked his lips several times when he spoke as if he was perpetually sucking a sweet.

She found it disturbing the way they would laugh behind their fists over silly things like 'Rahul knows how to plot a hillock…and a hump' while flicking the pages of 'topography maps'. Sometimes if he stayed for dinner Divesh would straighten his hair and collar too many times if Meena Mami was serving them. Reena noticed how Divesh watched Montuda's voluptuous mother and how Montuda found it amusing. She never told anyone, least of all her own mother. It would surely mean boarding school if Reena couldn't stay at Didun's house anymore. Reena considered his offer carefully. How come no one else notices their retarded behaviour? Maybe it was better if they shifted their Geography classes to Disgusting Divesh's house. Montu grinned at Reena's obvious disgust, but he knew he had won, he already understood the language of bargain.

School was the best getaway. There were so many other girls with so many strange stories you forgot your own. If she got bored with their stories she ran to the library looking for other lives to immerse herself in. That was her personal heaven, being someone else in some other place. Sadly library period came only once a week on Wednesdays and students were allowed only one book a week. So Reena made friends with the Librarian, a skinny lady in a long skirt. She promised to help in the library if she could take an extra book home in exchange. So Miss Gladys, the Librarian spoke to Reena's class teacher and her class teacher spoke to Reena's grandmother. Finally, Didun wrote a note to Reena's class teacher, who was also their Craft teacher, who made a special arrangement so Reena got to take an extra book home on the weekends. The deal was she did craft work by helping to bind new books in plastic and repair the older books every Friday during the Craft lesson.

Reena scoured the shelves for everything from mystery stories to historical novels. She read like her life depended on it. Miss Gladys realised Reena was dependable with returning books, so she got a free hand. Soon she gulped library books by the dozen, three a week, sometimes one a day reading all the way till bedtime. It was the only way she could stop thinking about why her mother didn't live with her. By the time evening came and the line for the bus snaked across the basketball field she got bored again. There was so little to do once she got home to her grandmother. She really needed to find a "bosom friend" like Anne in *Anne of Green Gables* had found Diana Barry; all girls in books had them. Even lonely Judy Abbot the orphan from *Daddy-long-legs* had Sally McBride. She needed to hurry up and find herself one. She was out there somewhere; she just had to locate her. Last year she had had no luck. So she waited to find her perfect friend, deciding that till then books would be her best friends.

This year she was full of hope again. Besides she was a teenager now. Life had to change. She was going to waste no time in starting her search. The first day at school and her birthday seemed a good place to start her search for her "bosom friend". Every year the girls were shuffled into fresh groups to form two or three separate batches for each class. This way the teachers thought they controlled troublemakers from teaming up. They also felt that it kept the students serious; preventing them from forming 'unhealthy' closed friendships.

Reena loved this shuffle. She looked forward to seeing someone new in her class every year. She hoped that she would have a pretty partner to share a desk with. She had read about so many best friends she could imagine exactly what her "bosom-friend" would look like.

On that 13th day of June she went to school in anticipation, dreaming of her friend-yet-to-be-found. She was fashioning a girl from all the accounts of perfect friends she had read. Piece by piece she had built her own abstract, but beautiful puzzle. She frowned as she jumped onto the old school bus, hardly hearing her old classmates greeting her for the first time after their summer vacation. She busily searched for a window seat. It looked like it was going to rain. Reena wanted to open the window and let the drops in. She tried but the glass was jammed down into the rubber piping of the window. She stared out and caught sight of her own reflection as a blue truck stopped beside the bus. She grinned at her reflection in greeting and sparkling teeth stared back.

'She definitely won't have braces', Reena thought determinedly.

The school bus was rushing into huge puddles of water, splashing the smaller cars as if it had a mind of its own. Reena looked and giggled but she was thinking of sailing boats in the open drain outside Didun's old bungalow. She'd have to sit and make them in break time from the pages of her new rough book. New pages always floated nicely; they didn't get all squishy and soaked as soon as they touched the water. It would be fun. During the Maths period, after lunch she got thoroughly bored. They were just starting on algebra and their new teacher, a youngish shy looking man, was trying busily to explain how alphabets could also be numbers. She glared at the black board, 'why can't the silly numbers just keep to themselves?' It infuriated her completely. 'Why do they have to ruin perfectly lovely alphabets which are meant to spell beautiful long words?' she thought possessively. Reena refused to listen, and began building herself sturdy little paper boats. She began to hum to herself without realizing it. Before she'd finished her second boat Sir Mohanan was by her side watching her deft fingers.

'Hmmm, ummm, hmmm,um!'

That wasn't her voice humming. She looked up and forgot the tune of the song that had been playing in her mind. Sir Mohanan looked furious. She was punished, to set an example that new teachers weren't 'easy'. She was happier of course, standing outside in the rainfilled corridor. She imagined sailing in a giant paper boat, with her best friend, through the lashing rain. She couldn't see her friend's face because her back was turned, but she was tall. The most luxuriant hair fell across her back in shimmering strands of black and deep brown, right to her waist. Reena reached out to touch her shoulder; she wanted her friend to turn. She wanted to see her face. But the bell rang in a piercing shrill.

Reena re-entered the classroom sniffing because she had been so close to seeing her friend's face. She didn't apologise, but stood instead with her head bent, hiding the tears that were welling under her eyelids. She didn't want anyone in the class to see her crying. Sir Mohanan softened when he saw her bent head, heard her sniffles. He wanted to cement his reputation as a tough teacher, but then thinking she was genuinely sorry he didn't give her the five hundred-line imposition as planned.

Reena settled back into her bench beside a skinny girl with bony hands. The classroom held no interesting faces, and not one of the girls had that glimmering long hair. Reena swallowed her disappointment. She stared back at the door that led to the corridor where she had been punished. It was empty. She stared at her partner for the first time that morning. Her hands are so bony, Reena thought.

She noticed her partner, who was bent over the algebra exercises, working quietly. Meera Naidu, she read noticing the sloppy blue inked letters spilling across the Maths textbook.

'Meera? Do you like Maths?'

Meera sat bolt upright as if someone had pulled her two-inch thick plaits.

'Huh? Oh...' Meera saw Reena's smudged eyes.

'Oh, I'm so sorry he caught you, I was concentrating on the sum and didn't get time to warn you before he...you're not angry with me are you? Were you cry...' She smiled nervously feeling immediately guilty.

'Ooh no! I just don't like Maths, I can't understand how letters can be numbers...it seems so silly.' Reena grinned sparkling her braces unintentionally, Meera looked relieved, she was afraid she might have to deal with an unfriendly partner who would blame her for the punishment.

'Look if you like Mathematics then maybe you could help me in the tea break? I didn't hear a word of what he was saying. The rest of the class I was in the corridor sailing...I mean standing still!' Meera smiled without parting her lips she looked quite nice when she wasn't looking worried.

Reena thought she might at least make a good friend if she couldn't find her best friend yet. 'In exchange I can help you with history if you like or English, I've already read both the new text books...'

'You have? That's quite a lot of reading. I'm good at Maths and Biology, my father and mother are scientists, but I hate reading. They both read a lot. Neither of them can help me with English or History, you know subjects that don't employ finite ideas…That's what Daddy says. Geography is fine, you can map everything, and there are reasons for all natural phenomena. But the minute it comes to vague ideas, it's quite hopeless. They try but… I want to be a botanist, so I don't need to… *you know.*'

She smiled at Reena this time showing all her teeth had the little metal brackets glued to them, which Reena hated so much. Reena grinned a little too wide to hide her disappointment and a rubber-band twanged out of her mouth. They watched it zinging through the air. Reena felt disgusted with her braces. Meera seemed to find this common ailment a portent of good things. 'Well, I'm sure we'll have more things in common, not just rubber-bands singing in our mouths.' Meera giggled. She sounded a little silly. Suddenly Reena wasn't sure she liked her. But she would have to settle for this partner.

'Ha, ha', Reena laughing politely inside her mouth, thinking she would never find a partner who was pretty and perfect at studies and as yet unattached and therefore willing to be *her* best friend. It was settled that both girls would help each other where the other was weak. They decided to work during each lunch hour instead of running around in the sun.

As the days grew into weeks Reena became more used to Meera's plainness. Although Meera seemed nice enough Reena was quite sure she could never be her true best friend. Each week she scanned the rest of the class divisions for other potential best friends. She settled down with a list of names figuring out if any one of the girls in the other classes would grow to become her best friend in next year's shuffle. When this got boring she kept trying to figure out if any of the girls with long hair fit the bill. She would walk behind them checking to see if their ponytails and plaits would fall like that, shimmering and wonderful if it was left open. Then she looked over at Meera's hair but it was only to just below her shoulders. Besides it was such a dull, oiled mess. No her best friend wasn't even in school yet.

Maybe, next year? Really being thirteen was boring.

That first month flew by, or that's how it seemed later. The monsoon winds blew the coconut trees in the city to stooping, and then a new wind straightened them up to face the sun again. Half the year was over before Reena realised that she had grown another inch and a half. Meera and she spent every break time poring over Math exercises. Then after that first term as partners every Wednesday after school Meera came over to Didun's house. There they would make a mock library and read aloud to each other. Reena taught Meera how to love words and Meera made Reena see the beauty of numbers marrying alphabets. Even if Meera wasn't going to be her best friend it was definite that they would be good partners.

They played badminton and Meera always won. She taught Reena just where to hold the racquet and how to step back balancing your weight evenly on your feet, shifting it gently first to the back then onto your front leg. Meera went on to become the badminton champion at school and Reena won the Scrabble tournament. They were so different.

By the end of the year Reena had scanned the entire class five times at least to see if anyone looked vaguely like the image of her friend. But no one even came close. She was already in the Seventh Standard; everyone had had a best friend for at least a year, some for two. No one found a best friend in the Eighth Standard everyone knew that. Reena began to lose hope.

Meera learnt how to write intriguing essays that summer because of the afternoons the two of them spent concocting adventures. Hidden behind a frayed *chatai* the two girls lived the pages of Reena's favourite mystery stories. The sunlight poured through the threadbare gaps and made patterns on Reena's wide-eyed face as she made believe she was Lorna Doone.

They played Scrabble, with Reena now keeping their scores skilfully, in the ramshackle outhouse cloistered by thick trees. Didun would make them thick glasses of watermelon crush and spike it with bright green mint leaves on those hot afternoons. The two of them sat sipping redness trapped in a glass, shaded by the cool broad leaves of the twin banana trees that grew in the huge garden. They were vagrant caravanners, gypsies with no homes, living on the kindness of the farmer from the big house. Didun was the farmer, though she didn't know it. Montuda was the rabid dog, tied to a pole warding off unwelcome guests. He didn't bully her so much anymore. She still hated him though.

Through that first summer they would pretend to be the people in the books they read. Meera was Diana Barry and Reena was Anne Shirley. And yet, Reena knew they were only pretending, they weren't really 'best' friends, like Anne and Diana had been. It was only a summer-time game. Meera wore braces and glasses. Her hair was always oiled and in plaits. Reena was sure, even when it was washed and open it wouldn't shimmer in the sun. She saw her one Sunday with her hair down over her shoulders, and in her mind she knew. Meera could never be her special friend, not with that limp lifeless hair.

To ignore her disappointment Reena began reading her grandmothers paperback copies of Agatha Christie. Murder captured her imagination at fourteen. She began devising the intricacies of planning a real murder. Montuda was to be the victim, 'a disease-spreading adolescent who blackmails his sister till she decides to kill him'. Reena's mind graphed unlikely ideas and she began to plot her first detective novel. Reena decided she wanted to be a writer when she was fourteen, but it was her secret. She read everything she could find. For a whole year she plotted and planned. She wove a new chapter in her head every time she had a minute alone. After six months she began to write, after a year she had a full-length story.

When she told Meera she said it shyly, her insides were tumbling. It was the first time she had shared something so personal with anyone other than her diary. Meera still didn't know about Reena's parents. She didn't ask. Reena was always silent about her father. Her mother came and stayed so rarely. Meera knew that Nayonika aunty was studying for her PhD at Cambridge University. It was Didun who shared any information about her daughter and son-in-law when Meera came over to spend the weekend sometimes. But she would tell Meera these things when Reena wasn't around; especially at night when Reena went to change into her nightdress. Didun would speak aloud, but only loud enough so Meera heard her. If her voice carried to the dressing room Reena would think Didun was whispering.

'My daughter always wanted to be an archaeologist, she studied Ancient Indian Culture at St Xavier's here and then she ran away to Deccan University in Poona...that's where she met Shomu. They say you shouldn't marry someone in the same profession. Archaeologists are always erratic, they shouldn't marry...shifty, very shifty...People who like to dig all day in the sun for bits and pieces from dead lives, must get affected by the heat...' She had no one else to listen to her version of things.

Then when Reena entered the room Didun would laugh, a nervous un-tinkling laugh, like stones being rattled in her throat. It was an unpleasant laugh, as if she wanted to actually shout and say something nasty, but her anger got trapped with the wind in her voice and she laughed instead. It was hearing that laugh that made Reena want more than ever to be a writer, to escape into her own stories, away from her grandmother's pain.

So the day Reena told Meera about wanting to be a writer Meera wasn't surprised. They were standing very close to each other. Reena was about to tell Meera about her completed detective story that she wanted to make into a novel.

'I knew it', Meera said proudly, 'You're so good at telling stories…' Her eyes had glowed like new leaves under raindrops. Their clear reflected light startled Reena. 'Your eyes are green Meera!'

Meera had finally lost her glasses. 'It was hyper-meteropia, the number faded gradually' Meera spoke quietly, almost embarrassed that Reena had noticed. Reena was shocked that in two years she had never realised that her friend had eyes the colour of the deep sea and emeralds.

'My father's great grandmother was Russian…he says his scientific genes and my eyes come from across the Steppes!' Meera held Reena's hand 'Thank you for sharing your secret with me. I know you've been writing something all these months. I would be honoured to partake of your literary effort madam…'

Reena laughed, the atmosphere lightened. They both loved talking fancy when they were alone, like characters in a book. That's how they continued for the next two years. Finally at the end of three years they faced the phantom of the final examinations and the monstrous prelims together. They prepared for the board exams chatting for long hours on the phone. Solving the last five-years-papers sets in three hours. Both were better than the other at Mathematics and vocabulary respectively.

Meera left Bombay after their final Tenth standard exams. Her parents shifted to Houston to carry forward some research. Reena wasn't very regular on the E-mail, but Meera remained in constant touch over the tumultuous year post-school. Reena was bored by her own stories, so she stopped writing and began reading to fill the emptiness again. By seventeen Reena finally stopped writing in her diary regularly.

That winter Reena's mother died suddenly. She contracted Meningitis in her final year at Cambridge; her thesis had just been submitted. Her father married a young film actress from Calcutta the day after Nayonika died. They tried to reach him on the phone, but his Bombay number was defunct.

Reena did not speak to anyone about her mother. All these years she had not shared her with anyone, she wrote her as many letters as there were days in a year. Suddenly she needed to tell someone how much she loved her, how deeply she felt responsible for her unhappiness. She sat alone on the porch of the silent house thinking '…if I hadn't been born then she could have left him, may be even married someone else, who would look after her the way she needs it. Someone who understands her…makes her laugh…I'm thinking in the present…'

She could hear quiet sobbing. 'Didun?' she wondered. But she did not want to go inside the bedroom and console her. She didn't feel able.

It didn't seem real that Ma was dead.

'Dead.' One horrible word changed a person from present to past. 'Maybe that's why they say 'passed away' no 'pass' is a verb.' It was like when Ma had left for Cambridge at first. The distance had seemed incomprehensible; she would sit by the phone willing it to ring. 'Maybe death makes that distance grow?' Now Reena felt like the distance had suddenly not just grown but become impassable, like a bridge had collapsed between two islands leaving not even the pillars to rebuild it someday. She wondered if she should continue writing letters to her mother. If only she had found her friend earlier in life. Who could she share anything with now, when even plain Meera had gone? It was only a year since she had left, but Reena felt like her days were suddenly longer and emptier than before. A week after her mother's funeral she turned on Mamu's computer and tried logging onto the net. The modem refused to function; it just bleeped in protest and irritated her as much as the stormy rain outside. After half an hour of painful bleeping and whirring she finally got into her Hotmail account and stabbed in her password. The keyboard was unused and the letter K always stuck.

There were two mails from Meera two days apart. One the day after the news had come from Cambridge, the next two days ago. Reading the electronic letter to herself she felt a sudden surge of excitement.

> *Reena, Just heard. You haven't written. Amma said I could take my annual holiday right away. Can I stay with you at Didun's? Is she fine? Look after her Reena, I'm coming this Sunday by the KLM-Northwest flight. It arrives at an ungodly hour, my cousin Shyam, (remember the cute one?) will come around to pick me up. He lives close to the airport...Look, I'm sorry I wasn't there. I soon will be ... can I get you anything? Yayyy, yay! See you...Sunday...Meera*

It was still Friday, and Sunday didn't seem just round the corner. She couldn't wait. It was still 8.30, she called Meera's aunt's house and spoke to Shyam. 'I want to pick her up', is all Reena said. Shyam didn't ask her anything; maybe Meera had spoken to him. She counted the hours to the flight. Didun was lying in bed. Montuda had finally been sent away to a boarding school in the south to improve his grades.

At the airport, waiting with anxious families Reena felt something she had not felt these last seven days. A terrible silence engulfed her. She would've been waiting like this for her mother. There were too many noisy children chasing after each other in a pointless game. Didn't kids go to school anymore, why were they allowed to be up so late, she wondered glaring at the parents who stood unaffectedly sipping coffee. The flight was on time, announced a disembodied voice. Reena decided to be alert. She was barely aware of Shyam smoking while they waited.

As she waited Reena noticed someone out of the corner of her eye. A tall girl had walked out of the arrivals hall with a single suitcase on a trolley. She walked gracefully like a beauty pageant entrant. She was wearing a deep blue sweater over pale blue pants. It was her hair, it was unbelievable. It shimmered with the sheen of dark coffee under sunlight. Before she could catch sight of her face the girl disappeared behind a group of customs officers. Watching her Reena remembered her vision of her imaginary best friend. It had been a while since she had thought of her. She stared at the girl whose face was now hidden by an airport sign. She could glimpse her bright blue sweater between their white uniforms. She was coming this way now. Reena felt suddenly conscious of her baggy checked shirt, she hadn't bothered to change; after all she was just going to the airport to collect Meera. She caught sight of the brilliant sweater again. The girl would walk past them in less than a minute. Reena stared suddenly wanting to reach out to this stunning girl. Should she talk to her?

For a split second she forgot who she was waiting for. Then the girl in the blue sweater walked right up to her. Reena didn't recognize her, till she looked into the emerald of the sea. The girl in the blue sweater came forward and put her arms around Reena's shoulders. And looking again into her bright green eyes Reena cried in her arms.

The Passport*

Vancouver Airport came alive around Rupin as he rolled his trolley into the check-in area. It was the first time he had seen the inside of their city airport. Airline advertisements and brightly smiling check-in agents ushered passengers toward the appropriate queues. Lining up with the other British Airways passengers he finally began to breathe.

All his adult life Rupin had wanted to make a journey. Here he was finally all checked in, sitting in his grey corduroy trousers, black shirt tucked in, his hair smelling faintly of Brylcreem. His wide fingers held a thin passport; the book that allowed you to travel through its pale pages to places beyond the snow. The red and blue air ticket was wedged neatly between the pages, marking the place where his leave to enter Great Britain would be stamped.

As a Canadian citizen he didn't need a visa, but he longed for one. Indian Passport holders needed visas to go almost everywhere. He had seen his cousin Jayesh's Indian passport, thick with smooth hologrammed visa stickers. The suitcase lying under his bed at home was stickered with coloured pictures of the places he wanted to go to. His imagination had been caught as a child when Tom had come home from Aruba with wild palms and pyramids pasted on his cartoon suitcase, showing off to a jealous Jerry.

'I'll have a suitcase just like that', he'd promised himself, 'and with one sticker for every place I visit'. It had been his dream, to travel the world collecting postcards of sunny places. Eighteen-year-old Rupin dreamed well, particularly in the day.

When the family came to see-off his Indian cousins he noticed hordes of other Indian families with large suitcases piled on silver trolleys. It had made him want to wander off with a happy looking family headed for 'home', somewhere away from this cold wet world he knew. That had been the first and last trip to the airport for the Indian boy born in Canada.

Now he was travelling, really on is way out of the airport he had only once seen the exterior of. But his black department store stroller and matching fibre suitcase were unstickered and would remain so. It would be cluttered, even childish to follow Tom now. Everything he carried was black. His dream would find a way in stamps and coloured holograms pasted on pages that promised to transport you anywhere. Trouble was, as a Canadian he could never equal the number of stamps and visas Jayesh's Indian passport would have. But this was the first ever stamp he had got, his first ever journey. He held the little leather-bound book tighter. The unstickered suitcase was probably on its way down to the baggage room, he thought, rumbling on a tired conveyer belt. Soon it would be swung onto the aircraft that would carry Rupin to the beginning of his dream. To a place where he could be Rupin Thakker, the man he wanted to be. The crowd in the departure lounge moved in whorls soundlessly, as Rupin sat lost in thought.

***

He was the middle son of unambitious parents. His elder brother Rupesh was an established computer software engineer, who inherited the traditional accountants' genes of their ancestors for keeping detailed figures and complicated processes in his head. Rupin's younger brother Ritin played ice hockey and was on the school team. Though he was sharp at Math, he was certain of his goal to be a champion ice hockey player or a rocket scientist. The family knew they couldn't afford to send him to an Ivy League college. So, determined and wiry Ritin decided to follow his dream and be a sportsman of repute, at least.

While Rupin read and 'internalised' Sri Aurobindo's spiritual teachings. Ritin trained and concentrated on building his calf muscles. It was true; all the men in their family had skinny legs. And Rupesh lived away from home, as far from their traditions as he could.

Traditionally their community was vegetarian. Eggs were the only non-vegetarian item allowed in their house, this exception was made for Ritin. 'Our Indian frame isn't made for such these snow games, but I'm going to do it…Ma's feeding me six eggs a day so I can be well muscled like Omar!' Their mother curried the offensive non-vegetarian things to disguise them in thick tomato-red gravy. Ritin said the white boiled eggs sliding about in curry on his plate reminded him of amateur skaters on ice.

The boys ate meat at the school canteen and on some Fridays with their father at Martha's Inn down the road from where they lived. Their mother suspected this hypocrisy though she never learnt of it from them. 'Perhaps partial consumption of meat isn't enough to build flesh and muscle' Ritin would complain. All Rupin's Muslim friends were thick sinewed and tall. It was possibly all that red meat. They were also the ones with the girlfriends.

***

Unlike Ritin, Rupin had never thought about his body or girls before. He sat hunched over his lean stomach, the folds of the black Anorak falling heavily on his slight shoulders. In an hour and a half he would be on that plane he could see shining outside in the rain, and on his way to London. He had been given a partial grant for his proficiency in Religious Studies.

Rupin read incessantly, unlike his brothers. He spent most evenings in their kitchen watching his mother work tirelessly at creating meals that took less than an hour to eat and over three to make. While she cooked she spoke like she never did when his father was home.

She filled his mind with images of Indian bazaars, and told him about cooking customs. They piled high in his mind imagining mounds of crushed turmeric, dusty orange smelling of just baked warm earthen pots. Rupin took up pottery at school urged by his mother to be more efficient with his fingers.

He sat sipping her words, with the honey and lemon tea she brewed with bruised holy basil when he had a bad chest cold. 'You must drink this every night *beta* even in London, *hah*? It will keep your sinuses clear.' She was worried for him, though Vancouver was far colder than London would ever be. 'It's a different type of cold *beta*, when your mother is not by your side to tend you'. He was susceptible to chest colds, and his mother's burnt turmeric root recipe worked unfailingly every time. Though the smell of smoky turmeric singed his nose like a bare lighter flame, it burnt the disease out as well.

It was difficult being independent when you lived in a foreign country, his mother said. 'People outside don't understand our culture. Women here work and are equal. But our body is weaker than a man...it is how we are made, so we must stay home and cook... and slice each piece of potato accurately, so when the men come home there is a good meal to strengthen his mind and body.' She never said these things when Ritin and Rupesh were around. They would have teased her. Ritin was as Canadian as their neighbour Nicholas, and Rupesh as indifferent as the postman.

'You are my only *beta* who understands me...I bless you with many sons and a wife who can cook with her eyes and her hands...that is my prayer. Our Indian girls are best, remember only marry a true Indian girl, huh?'

That's exactly what his father had been explaining to Rupesh who was now of marriageable age. 'Our Indian born girls are the best, I tell you. See how your mother cooks? She had made a ten course meal the day my father went to see her'. Ritin had eavesdropped and asked why he hadn't gone to see his bride himself; after all he would be marrying her not his father. 'You youngsters have no respect for tradition. It brings bad luck to see the girls face before the wedding night, my father chose her, that's how it was done. But they brought back a cushion cover she had embroidered.' He said proudly.

Ritin had made a rude joke later that night about unveiling a cock-eyed girl who brought luck because her husband hadn't seen her face before marrying her. 'Lucky for her huh? *Ah ha, ha!'* Ritin had a roaring laugh. 'It's all nonsense this tradition shit. Why didn't they just stay there in India then?'

Ritin was the rebel in the family. He would disappear into his room after school with his voluptuous dark eyed girlfriend. Their mother went shopping in the afternoons. Even if she returned while they were upstairs locked behind Ritin's door, she never breathed a word to their father. 'I need to exercise enough' Ritin would say showing the gap in his front teeth. Girls found him adorable. Rupin would spend the late afternoon studying at home, and hear his younger brother exercising next door, or usually he heard Rita. She had a high-pitched beautiful voice and large glossy eyes.

This was a secret Rupin knew; like he knew about his mother's embroidery. She had weak eyes and couldn't stitch, she was an excellent cook but it was her sister who was the deft fingered one. His father never found out. He also knew that Rupesh had had a boyfriend for three years and was planning to move to San Francisco soon. Rupesh planned to tell his parents only about the pay raise and the new job, not about the shared flat with Adam. Their father smoked incessantly, and carried a mouth freshener and a deo-spray everywhere. Rupin was the sober one, the one who brought balance. He believed it was his duty, his *dharma*. He knew people's secrets. They trusted his silence.

In the mornings Rupin and his mother shared a routine all their own. She would crush green cardamom, mint leaves, cloves, a pinch of spice dust, one stick of cinnamon and a little pepper into a boiling pot of carefully measured water. Into that she would add thick milk and heaped spoons of brown granular sugar and thick tea dust. 'This is the closest I get to real *jaggery, arrey* I wish you could see them churning huge pots of liquid sugar, crushed from the sugarcane sticks…that fragrance… I miss all that.' Rupin was hungry for pictures of the place she called home, her voice quavering slightly when she uttered the magical word, 'home'. Remembering her own mother's village, Rupin's mother would concoct the most reviving drink, *masala chai.* He sipped it and memorized her method, trying to learn everything she held in her neatly knotted bun. In London he would imitate her careful ceremonial cooking.

'You are the daughter I never had', she told him once, her eyes red with onion tears, or was it something else. He felt proud, most sons stayed out of their mother's kitchens, but he was his mother's Indian *beta*. Rupin watched her slicing pink oozy onions while a tiny pool of oil rippled at her elbow in a copper-bottomed wok. Mustard seeds popped under her fingers like heavy rainwater against wood slatted windows. She turned the flame up and threw the onions in, while another pan of rice came to a boil; she lowered that flame and kept cutting and cooking at once. Rupin admired her method. He would cook in London like that, like a real Indian.

***

The airport was noisy for this time of morning. Rupin rinsed his eyes, the water felt blue on his fingers. 'It's cold enough to turn my eyes from brown to blue' he thought. Three uniformed cleaners pushing cleaning carts brushed past him rudely. His heavy backpack lurched on his back with the impact.

'They did that on purpose,' he panicked. He immediately took it off his back and examined each pocket, constantly checking over his shoulder.

Rupin finally checked the outermost exposed pocket of his backpack. Nothing was missing. A slim battered notebook sat firm between his college admission file and Rohinton Mistry's latest novella. He sighed as he stroked the notebook feeling its worn cover. Rupin smiled warmly, like he was looking at his mother and not just a battered old notebook. These pages he held were filled with her many recipes, spattered in places with yellow *dal* some places with oil. When he looked up recipes in London he would be transported back by the many smells trapped between the pages, back to her kitchen where she would now cook without a helper.

But he wouldn't open the book here at the airport, even if he did miss her already. He wouldn't. It also contained a thick slice of India, his parents' home, a land he had never seen. Rupin inherited, intentionally, his mother's culinary equipment and constructed skill. He was carrying it now over the cold blue of the Atlantic Ocean to the land of India's conquerors. The people his father openly hated and secretly admired.

***

Most of the journey felt like a blur later, although Rupin drank minutes with their every detail. He soaked it all in; like unbuttered bread soaking up honey, his childhood imagination still sharp, still hungry. The September morning sun was a glow in the sky when he arrived, and the legend of grey London melted.

As he travelled from the broad Motorway leading out from Heathrow towards London the first thing he noticed was the narrowness of the city streets. These were not made for cars and two-lane traffic. The way houses were arranged around crescents and square gardens seemed like a child's model town set. Even the apartments looked box-like, more Lego-models than real houses, with rows of wrought iron fences bordered with bright purple and gold misshapen pansies. The same apartment stretched in an imitation of itself along a crescent. It seemed repetitive, almost boring. And yet because it was so different from the streets he knew he wanted watch and know it all. He decided, now that he was here he would get to know the city on foot.

The weight of neither his suitcase nor his backpack mattered as he tugged them uphill. The taxi dropped him on a steep kerb on the corner of the building that would be home now. He longed to start lectures, to begin the next three years of his life. He was going to study Sanskrit and Hinduism. His excitement rose with every step on the long road that led uphill to the halls of residence. It loomed ahead; a structure of pale brown clean cut stone. It looked more like a prison than a student hall. The first things that caught his attention were a pair of closed circuit cameras. It was five past seven GMT his watch said. The glass door leading in was locked. It looked so clean, like the glass wasn't there, un-thumbed by sticky fingers. Rupin was sweating steadily under the thickness of his shirt. The bags were heavy after all. He peered through the door. The building looked empty. He was too early; the office staff hadn't arrived yet. He had to wait in the damp green courtyard. The security guard at the reception read his paper intently.

'Excuse me?' Rupin tried to get the security guard's attention. He didn't seem to hear. Then Rupin noticed fine wires leading from his red ears into a tiny MP3, he tapped the tune with his pink fingers on the table.

'Excuse me?' Rupin tried again.

No response.

Finally Rupin knocked hard, his knuckles cold against the reception window.

The security chap looked up with a jerk, 'What?' he said, returning his gaze to the glossy newspaper almost instantly.

'Can't you see it's too early? Come back later.' The guard refused to meet Rupin's eyes again.

Rupin's shoulders stooped in sudden tiredness. He could no longer lug his heavy bags around. Rupin gestured at his luggage trying to get the chap's attention. But it was no use, he wasn't looking. Rupin knocked again, gesticulating at his suitcase, mouthing 'My luggage'.

'Oh, all right then!!' The guard punched lazily at a green button on his table. The door buzzed. Rupin pushed at the door with his shoulder pulling the black bag but too late, he couldn't cope with the suitcase. Suddenly it seemed to have gotten heavier. After buzzing him in thrice, the security guard had to come out of his cabin and hold the door open. He grabbed the suitcase from Rupin and said, 'It can stay here. You come back in two hours'. He slammed the door shut. Rupin stood staring through the unthumbed glass door at his only possessions in the world. The wind felt unfriendly in his hair. His eyes smarted.

Rupin wasn't the type to pick a fight. Besides he had been so excited. And now everything seemed terrible. The security guard was brusque, too brusque for someone so young. He seemed only a few years older than Rupin. But then authority did odd things to people's temperament. He remembered how Ritin's behaviour had changed when he was made Games Prefect. He had strutted like a male cat, all the girls giving chase. But he would turn and smile at Rupin with a wink when he passed him in the hallway, flanked by adoring girls, like it was some great male conspiracy.

This security fellow hadn't even smiled. Sitting on the dry front steps watching the traffic Rupin suddenly wondered about the next few years.

'How will I make friends?' He knew no one here, in this city with narrow roads and many one-way streets. If everyone was as unwelcoming as this security dude he wasn't looking forward to it as much as he had before.

A vague sound tumbled and echoed through his stomach. It was some hours since breakfast on the plane. He could almost hear his mother frying potato balls coated lightly in gram flour, to a gold crisp.

'I need something warm to eat and also a drink', thought Rupin.

He looked up toward the security guard who was the only human awake in London it seemed. Maybe he had tried the wrong approach. Maybe he should try again. He knocked on the window again. This time the guard was checking something on his computer screen. He had laid his earphones down. The window was slightly ajar. He would at least hear Rupin now. Rupin asked whether he could buy a coffee inside the hostel. Maybe he'd offer to buy him a cup, he thought as he spoke.

'Nope, no canteen in here,' the yellow haired man said, not looking up from the blue screen. His head firmly turned away from the window and Rupin.

Rupin attempted conversation. 'Where do *you* eat breakfast?'

'Home.'

'What if you're hungry in between?'

'Am not.'

The security guard said all this without shifting his gaze from the screen. His back seemed taut and unfriendly. Rupin wasn't giving up.

'In India they eat big breakfasts, my mother used to make them for me. I'm actually from India, but I was born and brought up in Vancouver…Canada.'

Suddenly the guard turned. Rupin grinned thinking he had finally managed to break the ice. His mother's cooking always did the trick. But the guard just picked up his paper again, without an upward glance at Rupin. Silence echoed from the black newsprint crowding the back page of the paper.

Rupin couldn't see his face; he paused then cleared his throat.

'How long till the office opens?' Rupin tried in vain.

'Told you before mate…may be two hours, or it may be more! Depends on Cathy,' he slurred.

'Can't I wait inside somewhere?' he asked, visualising a cosy common room of some kind with a television and a drink machine.

The unfriendly man nodded towards the bare bench out on the pavement, again without meeting his gaze.

Even under the September sun it was a little chilly outside. He saw the slightly damp bench that he was meant to sit on. He touched it. Wet. His corduroy trousers would be ruined. Rupin examined the building from a distance. It looked empty, the windows winked dimly in the sunlight. Where were the other students? Surely some other students must have arrived as well. His tongue felt thicker than usual. He began to feel a serious twinge of hunger.

Rupin's eyes were slowing, beginning to feel the length of the journey. He looked up the road and noticed a small, cheap looking café. He'd have a coffee there; it would have to keep him alive. He needed his pounds from his travel wallet in his backpack. He went back to the reception to knock on the window once more; but someone had just walked in. The glass door stood open held back by a brown leather suitcase. The air wafting beyond the door smelled faintly feminine, but not flowery.

A girl turned her head toward him, and then just as swiftly looked away. She too had arrived early, Rupin thought. Her dark head bent over the security guy's desk she was writing something. Rupin looked at the suitcase holding the door open, it was expensive leather. Then he looked at her other her bags, they all matched, all the identical shade of genuine leather, faun. A bright red and brown mirror studded shawl lay flung over them. The effect of sunlight and mirrors hypnotised Rupin further, he breathed deep of the faint fragrance that still hung in the air between them.

'You need to put in your personal details and then wait in the common room through that door there...' The guard explained before going back into his glass cabin.

'Okay', she said in voice unlike any Rupin had ever heard.

'SO! How do you say that pretty name?' His voice muffled like a badly tuned radio behind the glass cabin. Rupin couldn't hear him clearly, he heard only the girl.

'It's spelled S-a-g-a-r-i-k-a, but pronounced *Shagori*ka' she said, elongating the 'O' with her mouth wider. They smiled.

'We'll need the details of your course as well, the length etc.'

'Oh,' she nodded taking the form again and continuing to fill it again.

Rupin still stood at the threshold. He couldn't see the security guy's face. He took in glint of the mirror work shawl the dusky back of her neck, the slight built and said hesitantly, almost too soft to be heard, 'India right?'

Shagorika nodded again. She was nodding at the security guard who was now completely hidden from Rupin's view. The guard asked her to sit down. She sat.

Rupin thought she was nodding to him. He was breathing carefully again. 'She's from India; the first person I meet in London is from *home.*'

It went to his head like hot clove oil.

There was no one else in the reception area. Rupin felt more confident seeing her nod. He said, loudly this time, 'India is where I'm from too…' She jerked her head back and looked at him realising he was speaking to her. 'What? India hmm…I'm from Bombay actually,' she corrected absently, still writing.

Her voice was heavy and clear like a loud temple bell. She handed the filled form back and stood up. She was tall with short very black hair. It fell thickly over a small wheatish forehead.

He liked her immediately.

'Would you like some coffee?' Rupin asked the girl, he still hadn't introduced himself. She knelt on the floor, sorting something in her handbag. She pulled out a book. Rupin anxiously scanned its cover. Had he read it? Books were always a great conversation starter, though he hadn't been too successful with his kind of reading. It was a blue and black paperback, P G Wodehouse it said in white art deco type. His shoulders dropped, Rupin had never read him.

'My name is Rupin. I've lived outside India all my life. What's your name?'

She didn't answer. 'We'll have to wait over an hour for the office to open…' Rupin continued, trying to prompt her. She looked at her book, then up at him. She stood up to face him. Rupin felt shorter.

'Oh, what the hell…where can one get coffee in this place…?'

She was talking to the blond security guard again. He looked up from reading her filled out form smiling. His eyes were a strange purpley blue. To Rupin they had seemed a colourless grey before but now they gleamed, fresh pools of melted ice.

'We've got everything we need here'. It didn't sound like he was referring to the form.

Rupin felt a pang and said almost too loudly 'There's no canteen in here'.

'Yeah,' agreed the security guard.

He got up from his desk. He was over six feet and on closer inspection quite good looking. Rupin hadn't noticed that earlier either.

'The name's Alec' he added in a striking baritone addressing Sagarika, who was now standing with the red and brown shawl draped over her shoulders. Thrown over the simply cut black shirt and trousers the effect of colour and glinting mirrors was stunning.

The guard opened the main door and pointed up the street to the café Rupin had seen earlier.

'It's not great, but it's the closest and it's cheap. Don't expect frothy cappuccino or anything...' He actually laughed. Sagarika laughed back, a pearly half-laugh.

'Thanks Alec...can I get you a coffee...something else?'

He shrugged his ample shoulders and held the door open for her. 'I always get hungry between meals don't you?'

'Sure' replied Alec, 'but when I'm on the job…'

'Let me get you *something*?' she almost pleaded.

'Alright then, just coffee, no sugar, or milk' He grinned, his purple eyes mossing over, gentler now.

She smiled back, 'I will'.

Sagarika put on a pair of slim dark glasses and looked in Rupin's direction.

'Coming' she said. It wasn't really a query; she didn't seem interested. She wasn't pretty or anything, but her eyes smiled with her lips, at times without. There was something oddly distant about her attitude, it made Rupin want to follow her.

Rupin stood there, his mouth slightly open, wondering whether he was an unfriendly looking Canadian or if just meeting a girl had turned the security guard into a person. He opened the main door that had swung shut and followed Sagarika out into the now brighter road. It was beginning to get warmer. But he wasn't going to take off his anorak. She wore the shawl like his mother wore a *dupatta,* draped across her neck more an accessory than a necessity. He walked silently by her side, thinking of what to say; or maybe he should ask her something. She walked with large, confident steps. He watched her feet. She was wearing sensible walking shoes. Rupin's mind went blank.

He could only think of cooking. Then he thought of his mother. Maybe he should ask her about her mother. 'Do girls like talking about their mothers', he wondered.

No, Ritin's girlfriend constantly fought with her mother. But then she was Spanish; maybe Indian girls were different. Of course, they had to be different. Both his parents had taught him that. 'Only marry an Indian girl,' they'd both stressed. And the first person he met in London, at his college, was from India, a girl. It had to be a sign.

But Sagarika confused him.

How should he start a conversation? Trying to step in time with her large footsteps he wondered if she could cook.

'What kind of food do you make?' he blundered.

'You mean at home? Do you mean what sort of cuisine I like or what I eat?' she asked.

They had almost reached the café.

'No, I mean generally' he tried to clarify. Her eyes were shaded by the designer dark glasses. He couldn't see her eyes. He imagined her gaze would be cooling like fresh shower water on hot skin. He looked at her face; her eyebrows twitched together showing her confusion at his question. Her skin under the gentle sunlight looked smoothened like pancakes with pale sugar syrup. He listened for her voice trying again to imagine a temple bell, like the one in his mother's *puja* room. He imagined her pearly half-laugh from before, when she had giggled at the guard. Rupin wanted to make this girl laugh. What could he say to her?

'So what sort of food…' Sagarika cut into his attempt at rephrasing his question before he had formed it. Her voice was intolerant and rushed. 'Oh the usual stuff I guess, but I love Italian food. Pasta with basil pesto and also spinach cannelloni are my fave.'

'Oh wow! I don't cook Italian, maybe you can teach me', he smiled shyly.

'What, cooking!?'

She laughed, this time there was nothing half or pearly about it. She practically guffawed. 'You…*you* cook? I can't cook to save my life. Can you *really* cook?'

Rupin didn't answer. He couldn't.

'Then why did you choose these halls, I mean…there's no canteen and each flat has its own kitchen. So?'

'So?! I love eating out. My father said London has the best restaurants. He's made me a list. I'm dying to check out Gaucho Grill. Their pepper steak, medium-rare is legendary. Why waste money on stupid manufactured canteen food? No point staying at catered hostels. So I'm going to check them all out, The Ivy, if I want Indian food Dad said I should try Chutney Mary's... I will visit the lot. If I want to *cook* something I'll ask you.'

She laughed some more.

He stumbled, wondering about this Indian girl who couldn't cook. And she ate raw meat.

The old man at the kerbside table glanced up at them. He was balding and his belly showed under a stretched angry orange T-shirt. Pink and white paint formed a spattered pattern on his shoes; he was definitely a labourer.

Rupin looked into the square café they had just entered and noticed that most of the people were working class. 'Are you sure you *really* want to sit here?' He whispered.

But Sagarika had walked past him and already chosen a corner table overlooking the street. A bright sunny patch lighted the bean-blotched table. Sagarika pulled a few tissues from the holder on the table, wiping it clean. She beckoned to the plump motherly woman, who seemed to be the only waitress taking orders. She handed her the messy tissues.

'Good Morning' Sagarika said brightly, the temple bell tone to her voice was back. Rupin admired the way this girl could address anyone and disarm them instantly.

'Morning dear,' smiled back the woman. Her voice sounded far away, like an old song, 'What can I get you two lovelies?'

Rupin was about to order, but before he could Sagarika said 'I'll have a regular fry-up with everything, bacon, sausages and mushrooms, a fried tomato, baked beans and some brown bread and marmalade please... Actually, do you do fried bread? Ooh, yes! I'll have two bits of fried bread then, no toast! And black pudding please...just adore it.' She grinned taking off her dark glasses her eyes wide and excited suddenly.

'And to drink dear?' asked the lady whose blue shirt was really too long at the sleeves for someone who waited tables. 'Oh, I'll have some strong milky tea, English Breakfast? Two sugars please...'

'Right' o,' the woman smiled looking at Rupin, waiting for his order, her plucked eyebrows raised like Gothic arches.

'I'll have some coffee please, black. And do you have any jam? I'd like two slices of toast and an omelette.' She nodded at them and tucked her pencil behind her ear.

Sagarika pulled out a lean brown wallet and her book. She stretched her arms above her head 'God it's good to be in England…'

He didn't look at her stretching; he concentrated on the table, on the empty sugar bowl.

'What's black pudding?' Rupin asked.

'Hmm, it's congealed pig's blood…simply delicious.'

Rupin's words were a hopeless mess in his head. He stared down at the table again. His eyes fell on her wallet. It looked like it held her passport. 'May I see your passport?' asked Rupin suddenly sure of how to take the conversation forward.

'Sure!' she pushed the long wallet towards him with her closed book. He examined the pages of her Indian identity. She watched him. He decided after looking at her photograph pasted behind the thick plastic sheet: she was beautiful. It was a picture taken perhaps five years ago, but she looked the same, simple and pretty, her hair looked wonderful framing her face. It was a pity she had cut it. Should he tell her? He leafed through the pages. There were stamps from Thailand and Bahrain, a visit visa for the Netherlands and an interesting sticker version of her face on an American visa. The blue pages of her passport were thick with travel, and coloured stamps. His had the single leave to enter Great Britain, as a student. He fell silent, wondering what to ask next. He traced the stamped gold symbol that adorned the passport with its triplet lion heads. He felt a pull in his calves, and wondered about her family.

'Sagarika' He read.

'*Shagorika*' she corrected plainly, 'it's a Bengali name'

'Are you from Bengal?'

'No way! Mum's got this Bong hang up. She loves Satyajit Ray and *mishti doi* you know this really sickly sweet yogurt, that sort of stuff…so!' She glanced at him momentarily as if sizing him up.

'So how many brothers and sisters do you have…' ventured Rupin, still trying.

'None' said Sagarika and opened her book. *The Inimitable Jeeves* it said above the author's name, a fascinating caricature of an arch eyebrowed butler holding a tray of wineglasses filled the cover. Rupin stared at the book wondering what it was about.

Sagarika was guffawing silently, her eyes tracing lines in the air between them as she read. The cover of the book looked pale behind her beautifully manicured fingernails. A glint of pearly white made him realise she wore some sort of nail polish. His mother didn't, and Rita wore blue or red. She was really quite feminine this Indian girl. She was only pretending to be a tomboy, that's what his father had said about his half-Canadian cousin sister who only wore Levis jeans. Her dark glasses sat like a hair band on her head holding back her hair from her eyes.

He could see her full face. Shagorika, he formed her name in his mind, it sounded rare. He had never met a *real* Indian girl before, even in Vancouver. She foxed him. Hadn't her mother taught her how to cook? His mother had wanted a daughter, but then he had filled that space. After all he had expressed a desire to take on her culinary skin and carry on the tradition. He knew all the many Indian spices by name and smell. He even knew how to cut tomatoes into fine slivers for salad without squashing them. And yet, this girl from India? Maybe because she was an only child, that's it: she was pampered.

Their breakfast arrived. A ginger cat jumped onto a plate of unfinished bacon. They ate in silence. Rupin didn't dare speak again.

He watched her demolish the mass of pink meat and the black dollop of hardened blood on her plate. His omelette was warm and inoffensive.

'So where are you from Robin?' She asked, wiping her plate clean of the last red bean. The silence felt more comfortable. She put her book down and was looking at him.

'Vancouver, Canada. That's what my Canadian friends called me as well. But my name is Rupin. It's Sanskrit, it means one with a beautiful form'.

He blushed. She didn't blink.

'Rupin', she corrected herself. She heaped another spoon of sugar into her tea, stirring it. He felt braver.

'You can't enjoy that tea. I only drink coffee outside.' He smiled over his bitter brown brew.

'What do you mean?' She sounded almost child-like, her eyes wide again, her eyebrows spreading into her small forehead.

He explained like an expert, 'I'm thinking of *masala chai*? Like my Ma makes,' he smiled, 'just like your mother must also be making…'

'My mother? Making tea?' She breathed in a great gulp of her tea from the large white mug and said, 'My mother drinks only Earl Grey, made by our housemaid or manservant.'

'Oh' is all he managed to say.

They sat there the sun dividing them suddenly, distinctly into their own spaces.

***

The Café cat licked its bacon tipped paws clean. When Sagarika got up and paid at the counter, she and the waitress exchanged smiles. 'A black coffee to go, please, and a flapjack.'

*[Winner of Spiderthief Canadian short story prize, published in the winning volume]

Orange Cat

Eight months and three days since she had last spoken to Rahul. Sweat trickled from under her copper-wire frames, getting irritatingly close to her nostril. She clutched her files closer and blew at the pearl-like drop of perspiration pretending it was a strand of errant hair from her precise plait. Twenty-nine minutes past nine; she had been standing on the fast platform for over eleven minutes. She would be late.

Whenever she stood still she perspired, little bugging beads that she refused to wipe. It was too embarrassing, it always felt like someone was watching. She kept her hands firmly folded over the folders. Even though they would fit into her slim Rexene satchel, she preferred to hold something in her hands.

People were pushing onto the platform like waves of litter on the beach. The air also smelled like soggy garbage, despite the jostle of deodorizing odours from the morning office crowd standing under the yellow and red stripes where the first class passengers gathered. The humidity had risen. Eighty-three percent they announced on the news last night. This morning it felt like ninety-three or worse, the monsoon would soon be here. It collected in ominous grey clouds, but refused to break. Even if she didn't look at the calendar, the slippery film on her palms said it was May, and not yet June. She was longing for the rain, but right now just the train would do. She hated being late. This obsession with minutes was recent. No one at the office noticed if she was five or seven minutes late. It didn't seem to matter. But it gave her a great sense of satisfaction if she walked in as the minute hand on the glaring clock edged to mark the hour.

Perfect Ten.

***

When Rahul left her standing alone, in the evening rush hour at Churchgate Station, she counted the seconds. She watched the space between them grow as he paced toward the halted train, a sea of elbows nudging his steady form to hurry. She watched him heave onto the curved metal floor of the compartment. So many metal boxes of people chained to forever travel together. She watched but her eyes lost focus. He hadn't looked back, not once. 'It's over', is all he said.

His steadfastness had given her hope. He's pretending, she thought, he wants to turn. But he hadn't. The shrill burst of sound in her ear coincided with the flickering signal lamp that only a second ago had been orange, it turned soundlessly emerald.

And he disappeared. Everything went completely numb with quietness.

Suddenly sound poured back in. The railway clock above her head seemed to be ticking louder than the people. She had never heard it before. Sweaty arms sliced past her, and she felt the distinct weight of a fist in the pit of her belly. Maybe that's how it felt when you lost your first love, like water retention and nausea.

The next morning she set her watch to the office clock. Hers had been eight minutes slower than it for two whole years, and she hadn't even noticed. Turning the tiny knob of metal on her mother's aging wristwatch she smiled, remembering. Everything she touched sparked some recollection.

Their watches had been set to the same time, hers and Rahul's, not a minute apart, as if that bound them closer no matter where in the city they were. It had been his idea. She remembered the spark of laughter in his eyes as he set her watch to his, in their second month of courting.

She argued, 'How do you know your watch is correct and mine isn't, just like a man'. 'Fine, let's compromise. We'll settle for a time between the two', he said. Hers was three minutes ahead of his, so they put hers back by a minute and his forward by two. She had felt warm all over when he had done that, he really cares, she had told herself watching his fingers tracing the leather strap seasoned with her sweat, swollen under his fingertip. He had looked up and seen it there, that irresistible vulnerability of trusting someone with your time.

The next day they made love for the first time. Their watches sitting beside his bed on the steel trunk that served as his table. He whispered inaudible things into her, while trains rumbled by beneath his narrow warm flat.

***

The train still wasn't here. She looked up at the sky; it was the only uncrowded space before her. Three women T C's were comparing notes on how many absconders they had hauled up yesterday. They were standing so close she could tell which of them used perfumed oil in her hair and which one used plain coconut. Another couple was also discussing the evils of ticket-less travel loudly. She had just renewed her monthly pass. She tried to listen to the sounds inside her head. She'd been hearing strange noises lately; especially a crackle exactly like Rahul clearing his throat after he had kissed her for over thirty seconds.

'I should stop smoking' he'd say, crackling the air caught in his throat. She kept hearing that familiar crackle in crowded places. But when she turned around he was never there.

She looked away towards the bright metal tracks for any sign of the train. No. Should she risk taking the slow? It was always such a pain to decide, especially after waiting for twelve minutes, what if the fast came in as she reached the slow platform across the over bridge. It was fine if you decided immediately after getting to the station that it would be safer to take a slow, but invariably as it pulled out of the station the fast chugged in. Then while you sat motionless in a sluggish train at overcrowded stations, where you didn't want to be, the fast train sped past vindictively. She heard laughter and looked across the rusting iron fence to the Central Railway side where three children were picking plastic bottles off the tracks; she could see the clear brightness of the bottles. The bottles sparked back at her. The sound of crushing plastic reminded her of another hollow sound she didn't want to hear anymore. It really was too hot.

On impulse she decided not to go to the office at all. She had never taken a day off.

Mr. Mulla wouldn't be in till the day after and she was ahead in terms of filing anyway. She had researched the four cases they had on hand, two divorce settlements, one real estate matter and another difficult case of medical negligence. She was a fast learner and had picked up things in her first three months at the firm. That was almost two years ago, four years after she had shifted to Bombay from Guwahati.

***

Suddenly six years ago everything changed. Her mother died quietly in the night; that same week her father shifted to Bhubaneshwar to live with her eldest brother. She had never wanted to study law; she had no plan laid for her life. But then she had to make some decision, suddenly there was no home anymore. Both her brothers encouraged her to pursue legal studies. Her father too became unusually supportive. Normally the pressure to marry by twenty-one would have been crushing. But everything changed. Maybe it was Maa's sudden death, or the fact that the elder girl had married at twenty and was well settled abroad. So the family wouldn't be in disgrace in their tight-knit community.

Everything changed when Maa died. It was like the rope holding all the keys together had disintegrated, scattering them all. She wasn't sure what Maa had suffered from. They had called it a 'circulatory problem' when they spoke about it. But she didn't need to dwell on details; she saw the terrific hollow cough swelling her throat, and heard the wheezing.

Baba was a chain smoker. He smelled disgusting. Talcum powder under his arms and Old Spice aftershave behind his ears. But the smoke had got him beneath his thick, yellowed fingernails. No amount of deodorising could rid him of that acrid smell. She hated stale smoker's breath; it reminded her of Maa coughing in the room next to hers at night. She still heard it sometimes.

While Maa was in hospital *Dada* and *Chorda* managed everything. *Didi* flew in from Canada, where she was settled with her graphic designer husband and their five-year-old daughter. Then after the elaborate funeral everyone dispersed. When *Didi* left she couldn't stay on in Guwahati, in a house full of men and memories. She had only just completed her first year at college. So it was decided that twenty-year-old Shona would be sent to Bombay to Government Law College, where Ratna *pishi*, Baba's sister, would be her local guardian. Shona wasn't her real name, only her *dak naam*, as they called it in *Bangla*. Thanks to Maa it wasn't silly. Most of her cousins had hilarious pet names which they came to despise in their teens. Her real name was Rupali, meaning one made of silver. Everyone knew gold was valued more. When she was around four her meanest cousin, a sticky, thin girl with fat oily plaits had made her cry. 'Your parents don't really love you! You're only called *Rupo* and no one says Rupo-moni…that sounds so silly. If they really loved you more than your brothers or sister they'd have called Shona, *Shonamoni'*.

Those words had a peculiar sting. She had shivered with the effort not to cry, but couldn't hold off the hot drip from her eyes. She ran and lay down, flinging her tear-filled face into Maa's lap. She remembered still the distinct smell of ginger and burnt *hing* filling her nostrils when she clutched the damp folds of Maa's *sari*. Maa had laughed, 'My silly *Shonamoni*, have you ever seen me wearing gold? I love *rupo* that's why I called you Rupali. Mithali was named by your Baba, I wanted to name you. But you are my Shona as well…'

Maa had carefully smoothed her still short fringe her hands softer than her old cotton sari. She had almost fallen asleep, only Maa had to get up and finish cooking the *chorchori* before Baba got home at seven.

So she sat watching Maa slice orange peels off a pink pumpkin on the *bothi,* held expertly between her feet. A large plate sat patiently below the glinting sickle shaped blade, filling with neatly shaped vegetables. So many sorts, so many colours that would all lose their individual taste and create a new distinct aroma, like a family, that's how good *chorchori* tastes, Maa explained. She noticed for the first time the rows of silver toe rings her mother wore. Maa looked up at her staring eyes and smiled, 'You have a *dorbesh,* go and ask Maharaj to get you one from the *puja* room.' The *puja* room was truly a heavenly place, more because of the rows of thick clear glass *burnees* that held brightly coloured home cooked sweets than marble idols or silver statues of gods and goddesses.

***

The slow train going north began pulling out of the station. Rupali could hear the punctuated melody of a *bhajan* being sung somewhere deep in the belly of one of the compartments. It took people so long to get to work, why didn't they read, why didn't they like silence? Why yell, it wasn't really singing, just a rude rumble of unmusical voices. It was rude; not just toward those who didn't sing and or weren't religious, but especially to wake God so early with such a blare. What if he'd had a bad night? She couldn't help thinking of God still in the terms her mother had explained him in. A crotchety ailing grandfather, who must be appeased at all costs and fed well if he was to hand out any favours.

It amazed her when she first came to
Bombay, how people on their way to work spent
that one odd hour singing out loud. Chanting
accompanied by a strange jangling sound,
frenetic tiny cymbals clashing against each other
without melody, pushing the hymn out of the
train out onto the breeze. Now Rupali never
thought of God. Back in Guwahati she concocted
an image of him from the photograph of Tagore
in Baba's study and one of her mother's fathers.
When she was surrounded by huddled praying
figures at home in their incense-filled *puja* room
she imagined him grinning as he ate all her
favourite sweets, nodding and winking at her
conspiratorially. In reality that room had only
meant one thing to her; sweets. As the crowd
jostled onto the stairway upwards from the
departing train she gazed at the glass bottles
lining the long tea stall. The myopically thick
glass distorted the contents inside. Biscuits
looked like bars of pale brown chocolate, yellow

ladoos looked like a mass of uncooked *dal.*

Another memory tugged insistently at her plait.

***

She used to ask their aging cook Maharaj, for her favourite *dorbesh* while everyone napped in the afternoon. Although he made those beautiful fragrant sweets he smelled like an old shoe. She would inhale the scent of crystallized sugar while picking apart the round *ladoo*, destroying the mound of little red and yellow globes of sugariness. One by one she'd undo the tightly packed sticky sweet, eating slowly, making it last for ages while she sat under Dada and Boudi's bed. The newlyweds' room was on the ground floor tucked away from all the other rooms for privacy, but it got easily flooded in the rains. So Baba and Maharaj and Dada had lifted the four poster bed with its shimmering white *moshari* and placed two rows of crumbly red bricks under each foot. Whenever Shona wanted to eat her yummiest feast she'd disappear under the bed and pretend she was on a ship. It became her private, hidden playroom. The many holed *moshari* would be her sail, keeping out strong angry winds even if it didn't keep out mosquitoes, because Dada always had red bites on his neck, just below his earlobes. She would notice them always when he carried her on his back up to the *chaat* to look down from that terrace directly into the pond below, where the washer women thrashed mud out of their clothes. 'Boudi such big mosquitoes poor Dada, ask Maa for a new *moshari naa*?' Dada would cover his burning ears with his longish curls, and Boudi would giggle her tinkling glass bangle giggle. Dada would look away and smile; she never understood why he was so shy, till Rahul left a beautiful maroon bruise on her pale neck three weeks before he walked into the crowd at Churchgate Station.

'You're the biggest mosquito I've ever seen' she'd said without thinking. Seeing his confused expression, she'd told him about her eldest brother, his wife and their inefficient mosquito net. He'd laughed politely, 'That's so sweet'. She hadn't asked him what he thought was sweet; her thinking love bites were mosquito bites or her brother's shy smile over those feverish bites.

***

She suddenly longed to pick apart a *dorbesh*, but they didn't make them here like Maharaj used to, crumbly on the surface with sugar crystals. She had tried Sweet Bengal, scanning the glass cabinets for a yellow and red memory. She found it, but it just wasn't the same. She looked instead at the yellow and red painted in jagged lines on the iron bars that held up the roof of the platform where first class passengers stood. Those oily colours made her want to go home and cry.

Yes, she *would* go back to her quiet flat. 'Be alone,' she thought, a quietness spreading its butterfly feet across her eyes.

Mala wouldn't be home this morning; she was editing the latest promo they'd filmed. Edits went on for hours on end, and sometimes Mala stayed at the Editing Suite days at a time. Her flat mate was a film executive with a successful ad firm. She was a broad dark girl two inches taller than her. She always wore flat shoes, 'Gives the guys an inferiority complex if you're taller you know'. Rupali didn't know. Mala smoked and swore every time her bare feet touched the floor. They shared a flat with a tiny kitchen and a smelly sink in Pali Market, but not their lives. It was in an old Catholic neighbourhood, a cluster of sloping roofed rooms piled one above the other around a blue and white Cross statue.

The village housed neighbours who lived behind closed windows, but knew exactly what time you got in every night. Tiny red and green fairy lights flickered on every evening across the asbestos roofed courtyard covering when Paul, who ran the garage at Pali Market, turned on the switch from his first floor verandah. He was a lanky chap, all teeth and no smile. His eyes stank of beer and cheap cigarettes, but he was helpful with electrical work and fixing pipes. He seemed a good sort, just too fond of his beer in the morning. Mrs. Pinto, who showed her disapproval of unmarried girls who lived by themselves with her stoic silence, lived on the ground floor. She was always pacing in her tiny balcony across the courtyard from their flat. Pacing like a ghost in her black dress patterned with shining red roses. She would be at the market gossiping with the fruit sellers, discussing who spent more than twelve hundred rupees on mangoes this year. And Peter and his parents from the ground floor flat, with their unpronounceable Portuguese surname, none of them would be home now.

The hour hand on the railway clock inched forward and stopped. Ten.

Everyone would be at work. Rupali was now almost an hour late. A fuzzy voice sputtered over the speaker behind her head in perfect Marathi, she figured that the train was just approaching the station but was running really late. She saw its brown and yellow painted face growing larger and began to climb the steps toward the exit. She would go home and lie down, put some ice cubes in her hair, if Mala hadn't sloshed them all up with her Southern Comfort last night.

Mala really was unlike anyone Rupali had ever met. They'd entered the estate agents the same rainy evening last June looking for a home to make. Ratna *pishi* had been a careful LG. But they had shifted to Coonoor where her husband wanted to retire to, and Rupali didn't want to leave Bombay. She had got to know the city and its heady smells of dreaminess. She loved the ocean so close by. She would dream of it almost every night, the phosphorous waves lined her lips when she woke. She didn't really have anywhere to go back to besides. The job wasn't great, but she was gaining legal experience and might soon begin to practice. Mala seemed strong, and had already been living alone in the city for eleven years. She had to find new 'digs', as she called it, because she had split with her boyfriend in whose flat she lived.

Rupali got to know Mala, but she herself hardly spoke. She drew circles with her unpainted nails on the chipped marble they used as a table, set on top of a rusty iron clothes frame. Mala of course loved talking and never asked any questions, she laughed a lot and cried as hard. She came to Bombay to become an actress, she confessed one evening. She loved eating chicken and was a terrible cook, so Rupali would rustle up a Bengali meal every once in a while. They never met each other's friends and were happier working in different set-ups. 'So what's life like at the legal end, my little friend', she hated being called 'little', five feet four was not short! But she soon realized that taking offence to what Mala said would mean sulking every hour. So they got on. The good thing was that Mala was very particular about cleanliness. They never really entered each other's rooms; they ate in the triangular lobby between their rooms and the kitchen. Mala was the most uninquisitive person Rupali had met.

It was a homely living space. Mala had put up a few creepers on the kitchen grill and Rupali fit a mirror on the facing wall, beside the main door, so it looked like a window reflecting the creepers. The walls were whitewashed so they couldn't put anything up if there wasn't already a nail there. They left notes to each other on the small red fridge that Mala had got from her boyfriend's place, 'we used it beside his bar…God! That was an awesome flat, sea facing on Bandstand…imagine. I guess being in bed with the CEO has spoiled me!'

Rupali got into an auto and thought of sliding ice along her spine. Rahul had often offered to do that, but he didn't own a fridge. The hit song from the latest Hindi film blared as the driver crooned along tunelessly; she didn't have the heart to tell him to shut it off. Rahul and she had seen the film together, actually she had watched while he had concentrated on the buttons on her pale yellow top. She had been unable to breathe normally. In the interval he'd come back grinning with a softie and a coffee. 'I love softies' he said, and by the crook of his grin she knew he wasn't referring to the one melting in his broad brown hand. She had to stop thinking of him.

'Only thirty roopees, plees Didi', she hated red roses, but maybe she should start again. She stared at the face selling her the flowers. His big clean eyes looked so out of place on the street, framed by the redness of roses. He suddenly smiled, brighter than the shine on his nose, without begging her to buy the flowers and offered her a single rose. Her eyes hurt suddenly behind her glasses. She couldn't tell if it was the slap of sunlight or the fact that no one had ever given her flowers. She fished three softened ten rupee notes from her bag and handed them to him. A squelchy chocolate found its way into her hand as she dipped into her satchel replacing her purse. She turned to give it to the boy, but he was limping away. The auto bumbled ahead, and he was lost in the moving forms of cars and people. She unwrapped the chocolate and ate slowly, tasting it only when she bit into the still crisp wafer inside. She forgot to think of Rahul.

Thinking of a boy and the lone tightly curled rose in his hand she clambered up the steps toward their green door on the first floor. The smell of frying coconut and turmeric rose from the open window below her. She clutched the violently red roses carefully and began the climb to her flat. On the seventh step she suddenly stopped, an orange cat with deep green eyes was staring at her.

'Hello' she said, 'where did you come from?'

'Oh, I'm Mrs Pinto's cat, but she died last night, will you keep me?'

Rupali dropped her bunch of cold keys and punctured her fingers on the roses. She stared hard at the cat. He stared back, his eyes greener than before. Then a boy's laugh made her turn.

'Peter! Very funny...what do you...'

Peter was their downstairs neighbour's son, tall for his age and gleaming with braces.

'Sorry, Rupa auntie…but Mrs Pinto did die. We found her at ten o'clock today morning. Please can you keep her cat, he came and sat outside your house, he won't move from there only. I even tried to give him a fish.' He grinned, 'I like cats, but he doesn't like me…I think he smells Tony on me, cats always hate dogs…Tony is a good dog'.

'Okay…fine I'll see if he comes up with me…you go now, and stop staring.' She was wearing a knee length skirt for the first time, and from where he stood Peter could probably see right up to her unshaved thighs. She bent to pick up the fallen keys, Peter grinned with a flash of steel. She opened the door to the flat and the strong whiff of apricots and whisky crept along her hairline. She left the door open and put the flowers into the steel water jug. She searched the kitchen cabinet and found a saucer. Why does one instinctively give cats milk in saucers, she wondered as she watched the cream slip from the pan onto the blue ceramic plate with a 'plump'. The wide eyed cat followed her into the lobby and was sitting thoughtfully under the marble roof of the kitchen table. He licked his paws and looked at the saucer as if Rupali was late with his milk. She felt like she'd been doing this always when she placed the plate down. He dipped his white bearded chin into the milk and she distinctly felt he smiled.

'I'm losing it', she thought, adopting Mala's phrase. She lowered herself into the dining chair. She had been very silent. She poured herself a glass of cold water, there wasn't any ice. She sat watching the cat; its tongue was incredibly pink. It reminded her of those pumpkin peels collecting at her mother's silver ringed feet.

She wondered about Mrs. Pinto the silent silver haired lady on the ground floor. She had seven children who were all in different parts of the Arab Emirates. That's what Paul had told her once while trying to fix the stink of their kitchen sink.

'And Mr. Pinto?' she had asked.

'No one talks about him men, she's been like this only, always alone always old, right from when I was fourteen.' Mrs. Pinto apparently always wore black and red and sung softly after eight in the evening, when the night jasmine outside the kitchen grew fragrant. Rupali hadn't expected her to die. It wasn't as though she had been ill or anything. She had only smiled at her thrice or maybe four times. She always smiled back, she didn't look sad but Rupali knew she was, it was those Nat King Cole songs she used to sing. Autumn Leaves mostly. She had a pretty voice for an old woman. The cat finished washing its tail, promptly climbed onto Rupali's lap and began pawing her knees gently. She had never had a pet, but she stroked Mrs Pinto's cat like she had always done it. He was very quiet. He purred so softly against her thigh, she felt the vibration rather than heard it. His warmth spread all along her arm.

Suddenly she heard a low moan. She sipped some water. Was she hearing things again? Then it got louder, a deep throated satisfied woman. It was definitely a real sound, right here in the flat, not inside her head. There, again. Was Mala home already? A loud gasp confirmed that her flat mate was indeed in her room and perhaps not alone. A long series of moans and then a high pitched sighing seemed to end in silence. The orange cat kept purring on Rupali's lap. Then her heart clutched. After a deep silence she heard the clear crackle of air caught in a man's throat.

She was hearing things again. She tried concentrating on the purring of Mrs. Pinto's cat, so firm and real in her lap. There it was again that sharp sound like crisp burnt toast, just like Rahul clearing his throat.

The door opened. He stood there naked, stunned for a moment at seeing her. Then he smiled casually and called to Mala, 'your flat mate is back...'

He put on his shirt while Rupali watched the familiar freckle on his shoulder disappear under a layer of beige cotton. He didn't bother to put on his undies, the shirt was long enough. She sat silently, as he reached for the glass she'd been drinking from and poured himself some water. He licked his wide lips. Mala emerged from the shower her lips puffier and pinker than usual.

'Oh hi Roops, this is Rahul, he did the ad we just shot. He's great isn't he? Just started modelling, you're made for it baby...I can tell you'.

'And you're a born director babes,' he spelled out languorously, touching her waist with his fingers. She giggled and though she was past thirty-five it didn't sound awkward.

'Meet Rupali,' Mala was performing again, 'say –Hi- Roops he won't bite, or maybe he will…' she giggled again.

'Hi,' whispered Rupali.

'She's awfully shy, Rags… she's from a different line...legal…very serious and all. Hey you're looking great, I didn't see you putting on that skirt…what's that on your lap?'

The cat was staring at Rahul and had stopped purring. It dropped off Rupali's lap, went over to Mala and began rubbing itself against her thick bare calves. Water was dripping off her legs into a pool where she stood. Rahul glared at Rupali as she looked up from the cat.

'So, what do you do?' he asked nonchalantly.

Rupali's throat went black, as if she had swallowed a cup of boiling coffee in one gulp. She stared at his hands, a dot of pinched skin stared back at her from his forearm. She looked up at his face and saw a blotch of red on his neck, Mala was stroking it. 'Mosquitoes' she thought, her belly clutched again. She retched visibly. 'Excuse me,' she said and leapt up running to her room. She slammed the door shut.

'What's up Roops, you okay?' Mala cried, edging toward her flat mate's room when she accidentally stepped on the cat's tail. It shrieked, scratching Rahul squarely between his unarmed legs.

***

Rupali didn't hear any sounds anymore. Rahul had been hospitalized for serious surgery. Mala moved back into her boyfriend's sea facing flat, he finally asked her to marry him. They didn't really get married; she had just wanted to be asked. Not that anyone cared. Mala called Rupali to check on her sometimes.

The orange cat lived in Mala's empty room, as if he had always been there. Rupali smelled the night jasmine every evening and listened to Nat King Cole's swaying voice sing Autumn Leaves. The sound would float across the creepers and the courtyard, and wash into her kitchen where there were always red roses. She watched the song play with the breeze from the sea, while Paul's twinkling fairy lights, across the small courtyard, pretended it was always Christmas.

The Fork in the Road

Stormy. The paper lying on the unpolished desk looked too yellow to write on. He had sat unmoving, staring at it for over an hour. It thundered outside. Pale onionskin sheets glowed under the tungsten lamp, shaded as if by wet leaves in far off Poona. This was his third year in London. The light outside changed. Reddening like your inner thigh after the sting of a slap.

His palms were uneasy with warmth, his forehead crinkled under a single black curl deeper than his mother's thick hair. This was difficult. He hadn't replied a single letter, not even the registered mail from her two weeks ago. It was some eight months since he'd left home this last time, and he hadn't written to anyone there since he'd been back. He smelled home each time he sat at this desk; the distinct scent of crushed curry leaves spun out from inside the pages of his books. That strong smell had kept silver fish from trailing little webs of shiny light across the pages in India. It had faded over the last few months, especially over winter when everything smelled of cold steel and dripping water pipes.

He could suddenly see the tiny flat in Poona where he had no desk, where he had to work on the kitchen sideboard leaning against his mother's throbbing voice, trying to sing as she cooked boiled rice. The stink of sticky sludge that sealed the fragrance-less rice grains into a blob of *gulatti*, curdled in his stomach. Everyone here knew only of deeply fragrant long grained *basmati*, the rich-man's staple rice, though even in the bigger houses no one could afford it every day.

Why was he thinking of rice and that kitchen where his mother was probably still cooking in her chequered mustard and green cotton *saree*? She'd possibly be wearing starched white now. No green glass orbiting her wrists. He stopped looking at these images his mind conjured and turned back to the blankness of white paper under lamplight.

It had finally begun to rain outside the study window, beyond his dark head. The booming grew louder and he couldn't concentrate. It was all outside pouring down with the sudden burst of April, punctuated by insane thunder. Pelting spots of water ran down the muggy glass, muffling the sounds from the street three floors down. Jo was asleep. She was curled under his mother's grey *pashmina* shawl and telling by her smile, quite comforted by its certain heat. He saw her nakedness curve with her toe, peeping from under the gloomy weather. They had made love all afternoon. He had needed her. The thick whiff of menthol cigarettes tangled in her thin hair, the wetness of her eyes against his face, her hands both in their clawing and their stillness. It was difficult to bear. But he hadn't told her that when she'd grinned aloud, breaking the news while twirling his hair between her toes. He'd let her curl into sleep afterwards, hardly touching her. He couldn't see her face; her hair covered most of it except her pale pink lips.

London under scarlet April and sheets of unexpected rain was unbearable suddenly. He should possibly take a walk. Get on the bus and ride down the rain to Hyde Park. Drench himself in the cold breeze wafting through the white rock of Marble Arch. Then he shivered at the thought of the stalactite sharpness of these drops, he wasn't sure he wanted to feel them mid-evening alone, amid rumbling red double-deckers. Why was he afraid of this sudden storm?

In Poona he rushed out to greet the first gush of monsoon breath. He used to smell deep green while walking down to the German bakery on North Avenue. There he would order a cinnamon roll and mint *chai*. Sipping the hint of crushed mint in the milky tea, soaking the munched roll inside his mouth. It felt like an explosion of warm coloured scents, quietly. Listening all the while to the sounds around him of crackling fire-like drops, large and heavy on palm blades dripping emerald he hummed inside himself. Monsoon meant soaking mud sidewalks, fallen flowers crushed underfoot, and the air wiped clean of smoke from the nearby train station.

Everything here smelled different. Dirty, but different. The kerb where Grays Inn ended, meeting Kings Cross junction with its stench of too much beer badly held in men's bellies. That clinical smell of greying rain, not the murky nausea, that sprang to pinch your nose outside the Poona train terminus and its *sauchalay*. How odd, to remember home by the stink from the public urinal, but that's what he thought of whenever he passed hefty beer bellies spurting in the street. Piss didn't reek in this atmosphere of blankness; muggy tropical warmth seemed to heighten smells to their worst. But here even the worst was somehow bearable.

Why couldn't he think beyond visuals? He needed words, the right ones, but his mind didn't seem able. He felt the uneasy warmth spilling from his palms, as he slid them through dry dunes on his scalp. He had to do this. It was important especially now, after this afternoon.

Blankness. Unmarked white paper, he had to start writing, he would have to tell her.

Jo sighed and moved almost as inaudibly as the rain slowing to its usual London glimmer: not real drops, just drips.

Each time he left home to get the train to Bombay and its bustling international airport he'd cry. He'd board a blue plane bound for London Heathrow and whimper inside, but no one saw. He was going to leave it all behind, all the murmuring glares, all the un-mouthed accusations. Leave behind the small noisy flat in Poona where his three elder brothers rankled over grandmother's three-acre property and their wives meowed over mother's jewellery.

Especially his *bhabi* Anjali, with her large darkening eyes, her clinking red and gold glass bangles. She had the longest hair he'd ever seen, two feet of black spiralling curls dripping wet onto her paler back under a daringly low-cut blouse. The woman years younger than his

eldest brother Ramesh *dada*, madly attractive
even when she slit her eyes with suspicion. He
would forget the spilt milk on her red spun-silk
saree, the madness in her eyes when he had
refused to crease his own brother's bed. He
would forget.

Wipe clear the town where his father,
retired from the railways, had sat watching
trains. He would shut out his mother who never
left the kitchen, but for an hour to bathe and
pray, or five to nap at night. He would forget
trying to hand wash the milk stains from the
blood-coloured *saree* that smelled strongly of
Anjali who he didn't dare desire. He would
dump his dusty shirts into massive-mouthed
machines and watch them wash in whirls of
water at the bright little wood and glass
launderette in Chapel Market instead.

He stubbed at his memory with Jo's easy
menthols, which he had never smoked before,
then looked carefully at his hands. Their dark

well etched lines of fate were coming together to web his head. He looked again, glancing over at Jo lying there on his narrow bed. She sighed in her stupor to smile and curl catlike, almost protectively, about herself. She shifted and the grey *pashmina* slipped a little revealing her pale left calf. Ashok felt dark.

He would start he thought; start writing this letter to his mother. Write and tell her that he wouldn't be home this time next year. Write that he didn't want his brother's responsibilities to manage the dry fruit store under their second floor flat, now that father was dead and no one else could keep accurate accounts.

Dead, father was dead, that's what the registered letter had spelled out in his mother's clean tiny print of Marathi, almost like ancient brown Sanskrit manuscripts, brittle but not with age. What had he died of? The letter didn't say. She simply said he's 'gone now'.

Ashok imagined his father sitting outside the Station Master's square green room. His wide fingers dark from smoking a tightly wound piece of betel leaf, plump with pungent tobacco. His eyes darker still from watching his white smoke mingle with wider whirls rising from train engines. Watching the smoke from too many missed trains to somewhere he always mumbled he wanted to go.

'I'm not going to let that happen to me' thought Ashok almost violently, thinking of his elder brothers who had made nothing of themselves. No one expected him to be different. But Ashok had ambition. He would go ahead and accept the bursary that meant teaching the undergraduate History seminar twice each week, and forget the three arranged marriage proposals from 'good' households, all 'fair and tall girls', that his mother had written about last month.

He had landed the Felix scholarship to pursue a Master's degree. He had hardly believed it himself, Ashok Panditrao a student at the School of Oriental and African Studies, University of London. A Felix scholar! It was doing his BA at St Xaviers' College in Bombay that had helped, and the part time job at the British Council there. Through the Educational Counsellors he had found this way out. Out of his life in Poona, hemmed in by Anjali's darting looks right from the week after her wedding to aging Ramesh *dada*, and his mother's trembling curiosity. Her adamant concern for his own early marriage.

'No Maa, I need to study, I need to be someone who understands things.' Her voice had been calm but her eyes beseeching, 'but you already understand so much. You can tell the difference between seeds and fruits like I never could.' His voice hardened like a betel nut under hot sun, 'No Ma, other things! I need to understand things other than separating dried apricot from dried *anjeer* and reading train time-tables'. He had been laying out the steel plates for dinner. They never used cutlery, except to serve food. His mother's shocked eyes had filled with tears. Dinner that night had been too salty. He had licked his fingers clean after the meal, wondering whether food tasted different if it was shovelled into your mouth with a metal implement. He wanted to learn the art of eating with a fork and spoon. She hadn't spoken to him for twelve days.

Then there was Anjali, who always crept up on him reading in the kitchen when her mother-in-law went for a bath to their only bathroom. She would breathe against the fine hair on his bent neck. She formed the loose end of her saree into an arrowhead, tickling his burning ear with it. He'd flinch but never turn to look at her; she sniggered and called him 'half-man'. He glared at his textbooks, he breathed hard and held himself in. He would be blamed. He was only sixteen when he decided to leave, after the SSC boards for Bombay. But he had to wait a whole five years more, till after his graduation, to really leave.

And yet she followed him around, in copious letters written in synchronized Wren and Martin grammar. He hated the sight of those muddy blue inland letters, his name yelled across in a laboured sloping hand, as if she had embroidered the address on. Even now he couldn't tell his mother about any of that kitchen whispering and hand rubbing, justifying his slowly forming decision. His palms were still uneasy with her warmth. He should never have. He remembered the sound of milk bubbling, boiling over. Burnt.

Anjali smelled of *sindoor*, that red powder that whiffed like a mixture of fresh turmeric and wax crayons. She loved being different. Women from Bengal partitioned their hair into two halves marking a clear path of red with the head of a nail and then dusted it over their noses onto circles of Vaseline. It had shocked his mother, the red streak marking a path in her jet black hair like a Bengali bride. He hated the way most women in their community and even young girls tattooed their foreheads with blood-green dots.

He'd write and tell Ma, he didn't want his own past. He wanted to disentangle himself from his father's funeral smoke, from the *beedis* he smoked and those infernal monster trains. Those trains he believed had killed his father, breaking his heart because they refused to carry him further than Poona. But he couldn't tell her that. He would tell her instead how he had found this studio flat, rented cheap overlooking Islington Green, bordering Upper Street where all the offbeat exotic restaurants are. Most importantly he'd found himself, shaking from uncertainty about the way his life was flicking pages too fast.

He'd also found Jo there, one afternoon last summer. Rocking her chair on the street walk outside Gallipoli, her favourite Lebanese restaurant, with a halo of crumbly *baklava* around her. The sunlight had caught her pale yellow hair. She glowed like the sapphire coloured liquid she was swirling in her glass. It was an image of cleanness, like light bared. He had stared.

'Hello, I'm a poet' she'd said, carelessly sipping her Chablis, 'you must be a student of some sort.' She was so plain, so unthreatening, so clean somehow. He loved her, in the afternoons mostly, when she finished the morning shift at the Maps section at the British Library.

He would tell Maa that he had found himself. Especially now, at the end of his second year as a PhD student, with the clinching argument to tie his thesis in a neat pile. He only had to punch it all out on his second hand Compaq machine, fill in the investigative sections and sculpt the footnotes into a meaningful subtext. He had arrived; the offer for a Teaching Assistant position would soon materialize into a real job. He would write and tell her also, and watch her yellow stretched skin flare with shame and anger, that he and his white girlfriend would be having a baby in eight months or so. That he had a salary to support a poetess and child, and their yellow cat.

That he didn't want that past of rich traditional hues, fragrant with saffron. He didn't want a 'wife' who wore green bangles and black beads laced with a few gold ones, like a loose noose around her neck to signify that he was still alive. A woman who smelled like Anjali did, of boiled milk and coffee, branded a married woman. He wanted this that he had found. He wanted the grey unfamiliarity of this place he was just beginning to know.

The cold anonymity of this city washed over him in a gentle wave. Suddenly he wasn't so uncomfortable with this violent rain anymore. The translucence of London under glass-dust like drops seemed almost welcoming in contrast with the hue of home. Like that first summer he'd been here.

He had walked alone with the feeling that life was just turning from the flyleaf to the first page in his own private history. Walking down the fork in the road to Portobello Market on a warm glazed Saturday afternoon, he had rummaged among old things that people were selling. One woman had turned her entire household out on a single cart of scentless planks.

'Where are you from dearie? Studying here?' Her voice was soft. 'India', it didn't seem to matter. He had chatted with her, disarmed by her lack of interest in his roots. On impulse he had browsed through her cart.

Old books that smelled like his father's journal before the ink had faded, coloured glass bottles, a pile of card coasters with old car models on them and hand painted Indian scarves. Under those scarves he's noticed a misshapen silver fork, it felt sandy to his touch.

'How much for this?'

The brown tousle-haired woman with wide twitching eyebrows had smiled suddenly in her mustard suede pants.

'You have it fer nothing, dearie. It's quite old. I didn't mean to sell it, must have lain there with me scarves...but, what'll you use it fer?'

Ashok had been fascinated with the fluid shape of the useless fork. It was bent, one would never eat with it again, and it seemed weighted with memories. He paid her a pound for it anyway. 'Someday we'll swap stories,' he said. She didn't understand him but laughed anyway and pocketed the heavy coin.

He had come home and traced its shape, curving off the table, like the questioning brow of an angry woman. It was daubed with a lump of white paint on the cold handle. He tried to imagine where it had been, with a family of spoons and forks, knives and dessert cutlery, how it had gotten so misshapen, so useless.

He used to watch it for hours before he had moved into this flat, from the halls of residence, where he now lived with Jo. Earlier he'd talked to its cold form, feeling crazed and alone. He got lonely, writing at his desk all evening after eight hours of research at the library. His afternoons were now spent buried in either his research notes or Jo's tiny blond curls. Then he'd thrown it aside no longer interested.

Jo wore very little at home. Usually one of his T-shirts stretched out of shape by her Scandinavian body. She would come and sit on his lap as he worked, squirming to an inaudible song playing on her Discman, urging him to the floor. She introduced him to music and other things. She filled his mouth and his time.

Winter had been warmer with Jo in his bed, so even if the heating blipped off at 2am he turned his face into her swelling belly. He buried his dark fingers into the warm soft gold at the melting of her thighs, forgetting the sharp dripping of the ice outside. Jo would writhe with him, wiping his memory of milky coffee. He had begun to forget himself with her paleness all over his face and hands. That had been the beginning.

It grew faintly black outside as evening grew. He wanted to suck a mint; he could still taste Jo. He pulled a tiny gold curl from under his tongue. He tugged the lower-most drawer of the desk that came with the flat and breathed deep of its Burmese teak aroma, sweet and sad. The scent made him imagine where the wood must have come from, shipped over the backs of elephants, first lumbered then polished. So many other hands, he thought. It must have seen many writers through their worst, but he was having a seriously bad time starting on this letter. He thrust his hand under the three paper thick files and pricked his hand against something slow and cold. He smiled, remembering. Picking up the unsmooth silver fork he stared at it.

'I forgot,' Ashok said 'I have a story too'. He set it down as a paper weight, and began writing, 'Dear Ma, I won't be...'

Jo snored, suddenly.

Giving up Coffee

As I was staring at the blue wax dripping from the candle stand the lights went out. I wiped my glasses with every ounce of nonchalance I could manage. I'd never been to her house before. I don't sleep too well; I drink too much coffee. That day I gave it up. I'd only met her at Ranjeev's office and twice at Rama's place for coffee. Once I thought I saw her on the 83 home and smiled even. But when the girl stood up she'd been too short. It was obviously the length of her hair, or what I remembered it to be that had confused me. Thank God, I'd thought, because she hadn't turned to smile. Why are people suspicious of strangers' smiles anyway? This evening I'd planned to go to the beach as usual. Can't let the beach go waste now that I'm right here. In Delhi I never felt this drive to find wide-open places. All those tombs like the Lodhi gardens, surrounded with seriously tall trees, just sat there. I never went walking in the evenings, even though there is a park near GK II, the colony my grandfather's house is in.

Here in Bombay I walk on the wet beach every evening almost. It's a short walk from my PG place. There's this narrow lane that leads down to the sea, and it's always full of parked cars. I don't think I'll ever buy a car. I like walking. I didn't know I'd bump into Rupa or Shalini at the beach, they don't seem the type; more the gym and Walkman type. Both of them, separately, invited me to this Poetry Reading session by candlelight. 'At a friend's house,' they'd said. I'm not too keen on poetry. I think it complicates ordinary language frankly. But then, when Rupa, running past me in her black tights said, 'you've just got to be there'. I thought I would. Rupa is this amazingly smooth-faced Bengali girl. She's been at the agency longer than I have. I know she cooks well because we've shared her lunch often. She was on my list of wanted women for three whole months, till I figured she and the CEO had a scene and I was only the sub-plot. I used to try working late on evenings she stayed back, but the minute the other women left she'd cool off. Her eyes would stop darting at me when I spoke. I'm meant to have this incredible voice. Frankly, it bothers me. Rupa's hair and body are enough to give anyone an ache, but I thought I was getting somewhere till I realized she worked late for another reason only. I've been in this city only five months. She was the first person who was nice to me, and though the CEO stroked her neck and back publicly I always thought it was more fatherly. He is fifty-plus and he's got this hot model for a wife I've heard. Anyway, I saw enough on two occasions to figure he was more interested in the fingers that sketched the storyboards than the storyboards themselves. Rupa has got the most immaculate fingers. Just staring at them got me totally worked up one evening. Women's hands are more important than they realize. So when Rupa, her purple T-shirt hugging her like I wanted to, smiled at me through the wind at

Juhu beach and asked me to attend this poetry evening thing, I thought: why not! I was just crunching sand beneath my feet anyway, and the beach will still be there tomorrow. Maybe the CEO was showing her the top of his balding head too often. Maybe…something!

The perfume of oranges hung over my head.

Then when I stopped for my regular *naryal paani* near the Centaur hotel lights, Coconut water straight from the shell is a Bombay delicacy I allow myself. That's when I saw Shalini giggling with some twenty-year-old men. I've never seen her in shorts before. Though her thighs are quite full, she's shapely enough. She saw me and came up and asked eagerly what I was doing later.

It was already 8.30 then. Shalini is a trainee copywriter, still relatively raw for twenty-five. When two halfway interesting women ask me out to the same place, for a poetry session, well it's hard to say no. I'd be a fool to say no really, especially since I definitely had no intention of declining!

What's hard to believe is where the damned thing was being held.

I had no idea.

Here I am sitting, my face in the shadow of an old white bookshelf, watching Roshanara move in her own space. I've felt that calm soft silence inside once before. There was this girl in school. She was senior by two years. The boys thought I had the hots for her. But it wasn't that. Then I saw Roshanara.

She isn't madly attractive or anything, just simple. Sort of unpretentious, you know. If I think about it I think I can settle on her smile being it. I've seen other women in their homes. This one is different. There's no other way to put it. Her living room layout was all I'd seen of her house so far, and I could imagine her bedroom, as in her truly intimate space. No impure intent man no, no such thing! Actually, that's exactly how her small living-cum-dining area was – intimate.

Rupa and Shalini stood linked arm in arm, I'd never known they were close. Maybe they weren't, women are odd creatures that way especially around each other. I was looking at her house, the corners that she had created. Everything looked comfortable where it was. The shell collection inside a low unpolished glass topped table. They didn't sparkle; nothing was even vaguely ostentatious. Blue, there was a lot of blue in different shades everywhere. Every little corner arrangement made for a perfect photograph. The faint perfume of oranges was still in the air. She smiled toward me. She was talking to Ranjeev's wife, Malini. Her laugh, it wakened the air, it was exciting and full-blooded. It reminded me suddenly of freshly squeezed orange juice, not clear but thick with all the bits in it. She hadn't looked at me, only toward me and my little finger had quivered.

She was wearing a creamy lemon *salwar kameez*, the *kurta* stopped just above her knees. The shorter cut of the traditionally long top made her look taller, the arms of the lemon cloth were bare, and I could see her skin bright beneath the floral pattern. A man always has one woman he'll desire from a distance. He may never even speak to her. Just throw these wild unhappy intentions and never pursue any of them. But she exists in every man's life. Maybe she just walks by his flat door every morning, or he sees her at the bus stop. The first time I saw her at Ranjeev's office something went silent inside. I just watched. I'm not a believer in all this love bullshit, and certainly not at first sight. It's always seated much lower than the heart or eyes that 'first sight' stuff. No one bloody admits it that's all. I'm not a visualizer for nothing; I live for detail.

She was sipping a clear liquid from a tall flute with a pale blue stem. I couldn't see her hands; I hadn't noticed them before either.

Rupa's fingers wound still and long on Shalini's waist. They were touching each other a lot those two. I suddenly caught them both grinning like a pair of Siamese cats, looking over their shoulders sparking at me. I prickled and smiled back, adjusted my glasses and looked over at Roshanara again. But she had moved. What the hell was I doing here anyway? I had thought the poetry would begin earlier in the evening, I thought I'd sit around a bit and then *khisko* once I'd eaten. Rupa had mentioned *Biriyani* and kebabs; there was nothing on the dining table, only a couple of white lace-edged napkins. There was no poetry and the evening was over. May be I should leave as well, these girls were weird and however much I liked looking at Roshanara I could do it at home behind my own shut eyes. It seemed like a better idea, I was getting a bit sick of all this talking and no action. I was getting hungry.

Roshanara suddenly froze my glance by pulling a slim chopstick from the knot in her hair. The flood across her back sent that silent sensation through me again. She was now bending over the music system. Should I speak to her? No one had introduced us this evening. Billie Holiday's voice suddenly quietened everyone to murmuring.

The stage was being set it seemed.

Roshanara smiled, the kind of unconscious smile few women in the ad-industry spread across their faces. I immediately decided not to attempt any conversation with her. She had in any case crossed from the speakers, behind which I was standing, and walked to where the bald CEO and his hot model wife stood purring. Rupa was still with Shalini but giggling at something the floppy haired executive had said. I marvelled again at Bombay people's pretences.

I went back to watching Roshanara. Here was the woman I could see myself holding, not clutching and I hadn't the breath in me to speak with her. I played with my fingers and wondered when the poetry would start. The lights went on, snuffing the dim candlelight. Malini and Rupa put Biriyani and kebabs on the table. Roshanara brought out two large jugs of water; someone else carried a tray of clean glasses, watching her, my eyes went quiet again.

I picked at a chicken bone and breathed deep when she brushed past me with a pile of dirty plates. Cinnamon smells rose from the air around her. I put my plate away and began to browse the titles on her white shelves. A lot of film theory, some history, a few encyclopaedia collections. She seemed to live alone. I was imagining her bedroom again when I noticed several people had begun to leave. Rupa stood hugging the floppy haired fellow I hadn't met before. The CEO left, nodding to some of us, his model wife kissed Roshanara on both cheeks.

I felt a pang, and looked down.

So where was the poetry, it was night more than evening now. The food was all gone. The clear glass covering the shells was wiped and tiny candles were set on it. Someone put the lights out again, and the scent of citrus wafted past me. The stage really was being set. I noticed again, in the dimmed light how this woman took quiet pride in her home. There were many mud bowls, filled with fragrance-less white and yellow flowers, a few lit wicks travelled among them. Yet she herself was unfussed, an absolutely comfortable woman who actually laughed out loud. How old was she, I wondered, I couldn't tell.

I hadn't spoken to anyone at the party. There had been too many people in such a small place. Suddenly as more people left I could see more of the floor. It was pale pine; I immediately went to the door and took off my shoes. I don't like wearing socks and luckily my feet don't sweat. I noticed Roshanara looking at my feet, she smiled, but not at me.

Only a few people sat around holding drinks. Ranjeev and Malini, the tall floppy haired chap next to Rupa, they seemed suddenly inseparable, Shalini with two other men from the office. There was also this quiet wide-eyed girl, who I hadn't seen before; she sat her eyes staring painfully ahead at some point outside the door. Ranjeev handed out sheets of paper. They were printed in vague brownish ink; it looked more like faded black ink actually. Typed up poems, one for each of us, at the bottom of the page it read, Poetry.com.

Billie Holiday sang, I caught a few stray lines, *'the very thought of you...the mere idea of you...'* Her voice crinkled under the piano notes with real pain. I knew my jazz. It was odd that I wasn't more into poetry. Ranjeev cleared his throat and Billie stopped without a sigh. Only candles, smokeless and steady, and still the scent of oranges with a hint of cinnamon now.

Roshanara sat opposite me.

I glanced at the poem in my hand. It was very simple, and yet unlike anything I'd ever read. Pablo Neruda –Spanish? No, Latin American or something like that. I remembered him from *Il Postino*, this mad slow paced Italian film, which I had somehow liked, or was it a Spanish film. 'Metaphore' –hmm, metaphors...Roshanara with her flooding hair so comfortably curled around her silent easy face. I suddenly thought of taking pictures again.

Where was she from? What did her name mean? Shalini called her Roshan, Rupa called her Ross –I liked Roshanara. I hate shortening names. What did it mean? It sounded regal somehow. I wasn't listening to Ranjeev then a single line caught me, *'But I being poor have only my dreams, Tread softly for you tread on my dreams'*.

Maybe poetry wasn't so complicated after all.

'Anyone for Peppermint tea?' She asked, her eyes squarely on me. 'Hmm,' I managed. 'Sounds great,' slurped Shalini, she was sucking on an after dinner mint, which were being handed around. Roshanara left the room, and tinkering could be heard in the back of the house.

'You know that's the first time Ross has offered us her precious Peppermint tea,' Rupa was telling Shalini. 'She hardly ever shares her tea when we drop in. The weirdest thing is, she *never* hands a cup of tea directly to anyone, let alone make it for someone' 'That definitely sounds idiosyncratic! Weird man, but have you ever asked her why? We should ideate about it sometime…' Shalini giggled her careless trainee-copy writer giggle.

'Oh yah, I asked, she says it's a sign of intimacy, can you believe that?' continued Rupa. 'She can be pretty odd huh!'

Roshanara re-entered the room holding a clear blue tray with bright yellow V-shaped mugs. She was special this woman. Her personality stamped in the smells of something one can hold with closed eyes. She put the tray down and picked up her sheet with the poem on it. She read without the sound of breathing, like an accomplished jazz artiste. Unbelievable woman. I wasn't listening to her poem, just the voice. Wordless sound pouring from the faintly sketched mouth. I was glad I'd stayed back, I loved watching her. Everyone was looking at me when she finished reading. Had they noticed me staring, but she was stirring the green tea in its yellow tumbler? She hadn't noticed.

Then I opened my mouth to read the poem in front of me, but it was stuck. No sound. I gulped. Then my voice almost boomed into the candlelight. I suppose not talking much gives one a baser tone of voice, less used I guess. I read.

'And it was at that age... Poetry arrived

in search of me. I don't know,

I don't know where

It came from, from winter or a river.

I don't know how or when

No, they were not voices, they were not

Words, nor silence,

But from the street I was summoned,

From the branches of night,

Abruptly from the others

Among violent fires

Or returning alone

There I was without a face

And it touched me.'*

  She looked up straight at me and passed
me the cup of steamy tea she had been stirring.
'Thank you' I heard myself say as I sat down.
Her pale grey cat came and settled itself in my
lap. I bunched its hair into my palm. It purred,
or was that me?

  The blue candle dripped some more as I
sipped my peppermint tea and decided to give
up coffee.

*the first verse Poesia-Poetry from the Dual language edition
from: *Pablo Neruda Selected Poems*. [1992] *Trans. Anthony
Kerrigan et al.* Penguin: London, NY.

His Cat

Gusts of wind blew in through the broken window. Maya stood inside the corridor holding the key in her hand, hesitant. It had been threatening to rain again, an after effect of the cyclone in Goa. It finally broke and with the sound of pouring rain filling the narrow unlit passageway she entered the flat.

Sameer's flat.

She pushed the door open. His study; his home lay in much the same chaos, as it had been the first time he had brought her here. That had been several months ago.

Books dusty and disarrayed lay covering the floor around a paper-laden desk. The window was open, the rain had already been there, and the air betrayed its damp presence though it was six hours since it had stopped the last time. She stepped in.

The weight of his presence settled itself comfortably over her shoulders, almost stubbornly like the embrace of a child. Unwittingly she smiled.

Sadness with a smile to it, she thought, that's what he usually said, she understood suddenly.

She sat down beside the open door and took out a small journal from her camera bag. It was bound in soft old cloth, covered in inked flowers outside and tiny sketched ones inside. She undid the cord that held the book shut and wrote:

Do you think we could call ours a 'love story'? We never became lovers…I'm not sure we wanted to, or maybe we just weren't sure! How many such unfinished, half-begun, almost-there stories exist, I wonder? I wonder… And if they do exist then where do they all go?! Somewhere I'd read or heard maybe of a graveyard of dreams…Seems like the

likeliest place. And to think that's where this – 'we'
will belong, in that place of unfinished dreams.

I've decided to come to paper since there's no
hope of living it, not anymore. We've known each
other for what seems like forever. This is tough you
know, I'm not sure I can handle it right away. Better
get on with what I came here to do. Clear-up and pick
up the over-due library books and Cat and leave. Yes.

The sheets of yellow manuscript paper,
damp with the rain-heavy breeze, fluttered
slowly. She was drawn to them, as she was to
anything that had held his touch. His writing of
course expressed his person. Subtle, strong, clear
thinking. She had wanted to be a writer and
that's what he was. Maybe something among his
papers would speak to her, disclose an inch of
what he had felt. She couldn't ask him.

Still hesitant she touched the dark brown letters that seemed to grow across the pages. Her breath came sharply; this was the closest she had come to touching him. The broad, beautifully formed curves of his writing looked up. Maya almost caressed the warm paper, but listened to the alarm bell in her head instead. Don't get into something you can't deal with, not just yet. She ignored the springy sensation in her fingers. But the words seemed to whisper her name.

Words, endless, scrawled, bold and real, crowded the yellowness of the page. She longed to trace each letter as it formed from itself another and another. She touched the indented surface where the pressure of his pen had imprinted his thoughts, in words.

I imagine sharpened pencils, the way they seem so determined to write, to wear down the point of lead. The sheen of new wood, carved into slender hexagonal columns stamped by a German company, with a short eraser at the other end. It's still the best thing to write with. A pencil, long and sharp, not slow but well-paced like blood flowing in my fingers. I imagine my hands stained with efforted inkblots after I've hand written my immortal novel on yellow manuscript sheets. I want to know the origin of all words; why do we choose some over others. Why do we use words at all?

She couldn't read anymore, her eyes blurred. She could see only innumerable little scrawls, little words that held so much. Like this writing exercise he'd been doing, it gave her a clue to his thought process and how he hated words though he was a writer.

How much it had meant to her when she had got those long awaited postcards when Sameer had been away on assignments for the paper. They'd made her hold her breath, he'll say something, and he'll tell me this time. But he never had. It was never more than a word of personal greeting, 'Ciao Em' or 'Take Care girl', which seemed less personal written on alien photographic postcards that were always too bright.

Now seeing his writing spread like a tablecloth with fine embroidery made her want to leave the flat and bang the door behind her. She was left to deal with the smarting in her fingers and a curled up sensation in the small of her back longing to stretch itself.

The cat walked in. The window banged in the breeze and flew open again. Papers flew everywhere. She sneezed. Cat gazed nonchalantly across at her feet. Then pretending Maya didn't exist padded across to Sameer's chair and engaged herself in meticulous washing. First her paws then her hind leg raised gymnast-like, above her graceful grey head. Gentle lady like brushing down with the fine toothcomb of her tongue.

He loved this animal with a careless obsession. Yet he had never named her, like in *Breakfast at Tiffany's*. Maya remembered being struck by the use of that symbolism in the film. Audrey Hepburn's character had said something about her not owning the cat and the cat not belonging to her. 'We're just two lonely creatures, who belong to nobody', or something like that. Maya had thought it weird. Then she met Sameer with his nameless pet. She assumed his reasons were much the same, but had not asked.

Maya recalled the way Sameer would pretend not to really care. She had watched, longingly as he bunched up the snow-spattered fur, filling the wedges between his fingers. Settling then unsettling the becalmed smooth hair. Cat would lie absolutely still, paws outstretched in ecstasy, kneading his kneecaps.

He'd watch her watching his hands and gurgle inside his voice box.

'Don't you wish you were a cat?'

Reading her again.

'NO!' she screamed. And though her voice had remained silent then, she spoke aloud now. Cat awoke and fixed her knees with a stare.

Maya bent down to pick up the strewn papers. She could hear Sameer inside her memory. 'Cats are amazing creatures. We should be more like them. Graceful. Detached. Self-sufficient. If I don't feed her, she'll fend for herself. No doggy-eyed betrayed look if I'm late getting home. Cats are cats. Amazing, agile unattached…I love their disinterestedness'.

Had he been trying to tell her something? Maya rarely asked him questions. They'd been working together for almost three years for the city paper. He was a features writer who sometimes covered natural disasters and social awareness issues. He had been her oldest brother's best friend. She was a photographer with an ambition to write, which she had shared with Sameer over family meals. He spent a lot of time at their home. When she applied for a job at the same paper soon after her graduation Sameer had taken her under his wing. He was five years her senior, though not much taller.

After their first year together as colleagues and friends she realized he meant more to her than just a mentor-guide. Their Senior Editor was amazed at the quality of their first joint assignment.

'It's like she visualizes your word images. You guys better team up more often!' And that's what they had done. They had an amazing unspoken understanding of each other's work. She was a natural editor and was able to plough through his heavier material and prune the edges without losing any of the angst. She forced him to pare down his language and get to the point.

If they ever argued it was over work. He enhanced her need for expression by teaching her how to use an insiders approach while photographing burn victims or disaster survivors. 'You can't feel their pain, so don't pretend', he'd say. 'Just be one of them, like an Anthropologist…what's it called participant-observer or something.'

There was always a hidden jibe at her academic ambition of wanting to be an Indian Anthropologist working for an indigenous understanding of rural India. 'Practice what you've wanted to preach my friend.'

He summed up her ambition in his suggestions and she was able to delve into her own understanding of life and apply it to her photojournalism. He rarely praised her work, but after a shoot where they had not coordinated their ideas and yet their work reflected the same ideology she would notice something in his eyes. It was how he cocked his head slightly, and the way he silently looked at her work or gazed at her. But did that gaze say what she wanted to hear?

She had seen him watching her at work as she peered at her work, cropping her scanned pictures on Photoshop, enhancing badly lit images. He would look blankly through his silver framed glasses; like he was watching words take shape. Pretending to think, she knew that, or did she? The closest Sameer had come to acknowledging her importance in his life was at an office party when he had introduced her to some older colleagues as his 'partner'. Of course they worked well together. She imagined she was him behind her lens, seeing things the way he perceived them, seeing faces the way he described them, as people not images. Their faces were the landscapes.

Even apart from work they spent a lot of time together. It was never planned, but they shared most meal times together in the paper's amazingly subsidized cafeteria splitting badly cooked *biryani*. After work she began going to his house to help with longer features, which needed immediate proofing. 'I'm still too close to the material to be able to tell what should go and what shouldn't!' he'd complain.

She would smile at the irony, 'too close indeed!'

She'd return home late, but no one minded. Her parents were too busy with her second brother Sunil who suffered from severe asthma. He had already had two life threatening attacks. Sahil her eldest brother lived in Dubai where he was an investment banker.

Sameer and her brother Sahil had been in junior college together and had become fast friends. Sameer stayed at the college hostel not far from their house. In their final year Sameer's father had died in a car crash. He had seemed unaffected by the loss at the time. Maya had been quietly attentive and supportive, going for walks with him after the rain and talking for hours sometimes not at all.

They never spoke intimately.

'I've been told the men in our family are cursed not to live beyond their thirtieth birthday', he had jokingly told her once. He was twenty-eight then.

Sameer was an only child and had intentionally left Delhi when he finished school. He had been deeply in love with his maternal cousin Shraddha. She was half south Indian, and from all his vague accounts Maya could tell she must have been ravishing. She had felt a tiny twinge but had encouraged him to go back to Delhi and tell Shraddha how he felt at least. 'It's just one of those doomed stories, ended before it's begun…she knows…we…we were very young', she was infuriated by the way he spoke so little.

Shraddha had got married when he had turned thirty. On his thirty-second birthday Sameer had taken Maya to his studio flat, where they shared a pastry over a limpid cup of coffee.

'I guess the curse skips generations like genes should!' He had smiled his rare and comfortable smile. 'My father's ancestors were money-lenders. They had cheated some influential *Brahmin* family and were cursed by the wife of the old man who died from poverty. This was some three generations ago…that's how the story goes if I remember right!'

Maya had stared at his hands while he told her his reason for becoming a journalist. 'I need to work the cheating out of my veins. I write about social injustice and give or try to give a voice to people who despite having it can't or don't or won't use it…I need to work through my own *karma*.' That was as personal as he had ever got. That had been over three months ago. She hadn't come to his house after that shared cup of coffee. But they ate dinner together every day, like a ritual. That was before the earthquake assignment, which had disrupted everything.

Maya picked up the papers and settled them back on the desk. That's when she noticed an exceptionally neatly written sheaf of sheets. It was undated, and read simply 'Our Story'. Under that unlikely title it began as a letter addressed to 'Em' –that's me, Maya thought, her breath stalled.

Sameer loved shortening names to their first initial. It wasn't because it was fashionable, just easier. At first Maya had hoped it was an endearment. But she discovered another colleague Kavita Tiwari in the accounts department was called Kay Tee, and Komal in the editorial team was plain Kay.

She looked down at the teeming letters that ran across the lines under 'Em' and suddenly she didn't want to think. She was terrified. She didn't want to be here. This letter, this story whatever it was, was meant for or was at least about her.

All she had wanted was that he should care that she walked talked breathed. But never ever did he allow a single smile to mean more than 'Hello, it's you again'. Never any sign of attachment. Even their routine dinners were merely convenient. Her house lay between the cluster of restaurants and his studio flat. So it was easy to eat together without first planning it. He didn't cook. She tried to remember unassuming little words, stumbling against each other in the dark of her eyes. Should she read it? Should she? How would it help if she knew anyway? She dumped a heavy book down on the letter and turned her cramped back to it. It was too late; she didn't want to know anymore she told herself firmly.

Twirling her unruly hair into a tight bun, in an attempt to knot down her thoughts Maya began the sorting. Box files in a neat pile at her feet; paper cuttings into the red file, half-done assignments to her left. Long overdue books, humph…into the oversized duty free bag. The money would, she knew, be under the newspaper lining of his shirt shelf. Thank God the American Centre didn't charge fines. Those books were due back over nine weeks ago. Her own books, a thoroughly thumbed copy of *The Catcher in the Rye* and *To Kill a Mocking Bird,* which she had forgotten she had lent him and a couple of *National Geographic* issues. These she stacked on her right on the brown floor.

Then his bedside table, what a mess! It hurt her to check his old work. Proofs she had scribbled notes on, abandoned feature ideas, doodles on possible interviews. Gathering up the stray sheets of his spilled mind she fought hard not to read…not to think how his fingers must have curled to hold the pen. Where was it, his immortal Mont Blanc?

She glanced over the now neater room. How unlike him it looked, with no shirts hung carelessly on the door or flung over the chair, smelly socks hidden under a pile of books, long forgotten, no longer sticky from the heat of his body. She didn't want to think; not of his fingers on the silver pen or his toes inside grey socks. He was eccentric that way; he only wore a pair of socks once, and then threw them away. He was truly a writer; he just had to find that story inside him. Stop thinking, just stop, her mind rumbled.

But then maybe it was better to think it through, and finally will it out of her system. Remember, remember she willed herself.

How must he have sat at this desk? Quiet, late into the night, hunched over yellow papered legal pads. He only wrote on yellow lined paper, and she was always sent hunting for them in the legal stationers. She imagined the pale glow of those sheets showing up reflected on his face while he groped for good pieces. Doing then redoing tail ends. Pausing to think in the midst of an article, the light playing on the edge of his glasses, his forehead lightly creased. His eyes grown softer from long hours of thinking and research. The slow movement of his fingers over his temple, rubbing lightly, gently going back and forth as if wiping his mind of dust. His hair showing up gold flecked under the brightness of the green shaded lamp.

The end of Maya's neck sat heavy on her spine. Suddenly she couldn't bear it any more. She decided to face it. She turned to the desk where she had imagined him at work. She leant over Cat, lifted the heavy encyclopaedia and picked up the letter that whispered '*Em*' on the red margin of the paper.

He would never know anyhow. Cat would be hers now. She would pay the rent, move out of her parents' house like she had planned for years, and return her books to the library before they were due. She'd take her pictures of car crashes and earthquakes like nothing had ever mattered. Like the rain fell, slow then steadier, growing heavy then heavier like her head. She looked the letter full in the face.

Em,

I'm going to try, finally try, to tell you. I'm not sure what exactly I wanted to say, but here it is all the same. After you left the other day I could smell you here in this room. I thought I'd go crazy. I had to leave all the windows open for the night. I wouldn't have been able to sleep with that whiff of you still floating about. Then the smell of the garbage from outside almost erased it, but I could still sense you. I thought I'd sleep. I didn't, not a wink. I sat up and wrote two pieces that I don't think will ever see the light of day.

How long have we known each other Maya? It seems like I remember your face at eight. Did we meet then? But that happens when I've been staring at your hair too long. I watch you so often, like Cat. Cat watches you too, have you noticed? Maybe she's jealous. I should stop. I pretend to be thinking sometimes when you look up and catch me watching you.

I'm meant to be a writer and I can't even begin to describe what you make me feel. After I left home and Delhi I've never wanted to hold someone at night. You make me want to burn this empty room and share a pillow. I want to see you asleep before I start working at night at this desk. I want to be able to watch you while I work on my novel, and to be woken by your smell on my face. The curve of your smile reminds me of sailing paper boats in the tank outside my grandmother's house.

I didn't realize I don't talk about myself, that I frown when I eat, that I'm a lonely bastard. You've never told me any of this either, but when you left tonight I felt it all. It's just the way you smile at me when you leave.

Incomplete.

Maya stood in absolute silence. Her fingers closed tighter round the edge of the paper, collapsing onto themselves. Exactly like a month ago when Arun the Senior Editor had walked up to her and her fingers had unwilling crushed her best portraits of earthquake survivors fresh off the train at Bombay Central listening to him droning. Arun's grim voice had finally cut into her neck.

'Maya. I'm afraid...there was an accident. During rescue work at Bhuj last evening a building collapsed. The team was digging a woman and her child out. She's safe. Sameer died before they could reach the hospital camp. Are you okay?'

She hadn't heard half of what he said later. Strange disjoint sentences. How did one face death? The photographs of devastated faces stared up at her from the circle they'd formed around her feet. Those people had lost so much; entire families, homes, everything they owned, even their identity. She looked down at the faces she had tried to capture yesterday and stood trapped. She couldn't step out. Her calves felt like thick cold meat. The face of an old man, deep eyes staring out –so black they almost looked purple. She kept staring at him, while the other faces crowded her in.

Now she stood, Sameer's writing lifting off the ground in a swirl around her. That same trapped feeling crowded her throat.

She picked up Cat and shut the window to the wind. But she could still hear the rain, as the papers floated down.

Rain fell, and filled the silence.

Orange Rosebuds in August

August, month of the sun. This one Sunday in August, when the rosebuds I bought actually bloomed in my living room, some memory bloomed alongside.

So orange like this month of the sun and radiant, almost rustily so. It was magical how a colour transferred its texture to a seasonal phase of the year, just before autumn set in. Fleetingly. Turning over too soon to allow the cold of London winter to bleed that orange to nothing but splinters of rain.

Muddied leaves lying along Gower Street squelching under wheels in matted miles. While the red 73 hummed, its passengers wrapped in tungsten on their way to Oxford Street and all its hurrying. The cold seeped through my twenty-pound jacket under the loose wool layer of the maroon scarf, tickling my bones to discomfort as I walked home. That place I lived in, hidden under the older part of Kings Cross, alongside the flaming St Pancras building: reminder of a stranger age in architecture. Everywhere was swabbed by a wet breeze, heavy with colder promises.

No one else bought the orange rosebuds that day. I don't know why I picked them out at the covered market early that Sunday morning. They seemed to remind me of something. I couldn't tell what.

The youngish woman, in her beige clean cut suit of Chinese fibres, said they looked too bright for blue and white living rooms. Possibly furnished in pale pine, smelling of blanched yesterdays spent dreaming. What was it she'd said, a shrug in her voice, 'they'll threaten the silence'. I've always wondered if cut flowers will survive longer than a few hours in stranger's houses. First in chipped enamel water jugs, then in Habitat vases of blue glass. Perhaps in green bottles that still whiff of brown wine or pint glasses burping from last night's beer, depending of course where on this city's crawling map that house is.

Looking at the orange unfurling of the buds surrounded by the softer sprinkle of baby's breath that I saved three bunches of, however, I realize I may allow myself to love me. No one has done so in a while.

I wish it were romantic love though, not self-love all philosophic and pristine. Love. The real durable kind in Celtic churches somewhere west of here. Marrying him, the longhaired one, in secret. It had to be that way in Scotland then. It couldn't be known in the village or anywhere. Or the soldiers would come to claim their share of me on my wedding night. The smirking English soldiers their reins never quite in hand, digging gleeful spurred boots into the muscled sides of chestnut mares. So we ran away, the longhaired one and I. We walked a day and a half, then longer. I lost count of those sunless hours, growing longer, still smelling the fading floral breeze. It was hard not to pick the fallen flowers for pressing, swathed in muslin under rocks. Sweet William and the little yellow tufts that sat on the gorse bushes like butterflies made of butter. Press their faces and their particular perfume, then churn them into the hot wax that father wove into scented candles. Sealing them forever, till someone else put flame to the petals frozen in wax to set their fragrant breath free. He would have to do it all, alone now that I was gone over the hills toward West Wales holding the wind in my flower-free wax stained hands. Father with his age in his eyes and me with too many dreams like chains of daisies and wide-eyed Susannah's tangled in my hair, browned from lying too long under a hurrying sun. So we walked, the longhaired one and I, mostly silent but smiling. I was afraid to know his name. It would mean betraying him if we were captured. Myself I didn't trust. In my mind I called him *Windfire*, for my midnight silences. I knew his eyes well though. The light from fathers candles in their darkness, showing me the bottomlessness of their pools. I stared deep, memorising the faint creases under their lashes that deepened each time he laughed. Each time we dared press the air with sound, the half wood outside resounded with his thick laugh, oiled and beautiful. We knew each other in silence always. It was better to move soundlessly, the night in ones loosely sewn shoes of strapped leather. He would come often, after the houses and their kitchens had fallen silent, and we could hear only the unlit branches whispering among themselves. In winter the scratching bareness of those branches scared me, and I'd wait for him to climb across the wide window. We'd watch each other in that glimmering of melting wax and pressed fragrances, just watch in a silence more knotted than the one in my ears now. It was so dark without the moon sometimes, soaked in cloud vapour. I wished I had brought one or two of fathers' thick candles that held as much light as wax and also smells of home. That place we were leaving farther behind our pacing backs. Somehow we wove our way through dim birch paths and old oak leaves at our feet. It was his eyes always leading us through the thickest darkness, because we couldn't run by day, those wild bright eyes that were never silent. He cried pearls into my hair that night when we married. Finally, in the Welsh chapel at the hillside, hidden, our Nevern chapel, with no priest but the moonlit cross of angels. I cried too, but later. I wanted him to think I was brave. It was so important to cry silently then. We had walked for almost a fortnight, watching the waxing moon. The edges of his uncut fingernails brushed my cheeks to flushes under the billowing moon. It wasn't full yet, though I wanted it to be. It shone half-risen and yellow over the white coarseness of cloth, draped on the stone table under the cross. He held my waist when it was over, our binding kiss of many life times ago, gently. I think he thought I would snap. He held me so gently, he did seem afraid telling by his quickening breath on my skin. I was strong, I know I was, caught in that trembling moment of us. I felt his palms uncreased like lake-water on my arms. I heard the low call of a cricket somewhere in the dark air under the rowed pews; it transformed into pipes of music curling into his shoulder length hair. That was when I noticed the sudden rustiness of colour on the unembroidered cloth. So inhumanly orange like nothing I'd seen before. Those opening buds smelled faintly like old roses trapped in the dark. They were like winter fire caught in my hair he said; embers of some other time perhaps an autumn evening like this one. August entwined in ribbons of deepening tangerine light, like an unquenched fireplace. He touched his eyes to my lips still moist with his wetness. I was unafraid to love him in that massive sanctuary of the moon, slanting through coloured slats of glass. When I stood naked I didn't shiver in the silence under that light, spinning pictures of long ago. How old was he, my husband of wind and fire. Lighting light with the sword now tightly sheathed silenced

without moonlight. Deft with his feet which
were now nestling my toes to warmth. I wanted
only to look at his face when he filled me with a
happiness I'd never sensed in my stomach
before. I moaned, still hearing the panpipes over
our forms, sculpting their shield of music above
us. His hair smudging my face whispered with
the glow of scented wax that burns in a low pool
on the floor. In that place of stone brickwork and
metallurgy we worshipped each the other.
Shaping ourselves into one note of music
wrought of wind with deep red fire.

I remember all this so clearly this August
so far away, untouched by the sound of
panpipes or wind fuelling fire. Here in this city
where I live alone with my cut flowers, selling
them every day at the street market for three
pounds or less if I like their faces. My cart of
wizened planks between Sarah the clean quiet
fruit-seller and the wise eyed vegetable chap
Thomas whose unchanged shirt, the colour of
soggy spinach, smells. There opposite the
sweeter smelling propped tent of the man
without a neck. He sells herb and fruit teas of all
competing fragrances a few pence cheaper than
Sainsburys', or that's what his regulars believe.
When they come to Chapel market by Angel
tube station on the black Northern line I wonder
how long they'll last without plant food, hardly
any sun in thickly draped shut houses. In some
perhaps longer than in others, someone with a
curling white apron will remember to change the
water every few days and trim the rotting stems.

But others like the shut unseeing windows will forget. Trying so hard to trap the warmth indoors. Too hard almost, snapping their stems instead. I play games with those faces, trying to tell which of them will return within the week for a fresh bunch of the same variety that they killed six days ago. Sometimes they don't come back, and rob my game of playing pieces. Sometimes they remember to smile when they see the colour they wish was reflected in someone who is locked up at home. I'd rather they didn't thank me though because I don't grow them, I don't pluck them either. I just buy the ones I like best from the wholesaler earlier than the others because I only have to leave a saucer of milk out for Tobias, the silly ginger cat that visits me before I walk the city at six. I have no household chores, neither is there anyone to breakfast with, so there's no washing, no chopping to prepare a lunch in the morning. No children to be sent to school on time, faces brushed and noses shining. It's just me; my cup of weakened tea from saved tea bags and his saucer of milk throwing up warm curls of air. It's my colourless face they will recall when they need to buy flowers again, perhaps for an office mate's birthday dinner. Then maybe a flower woman has no face in someone else's memory.

But no one bought the tightly curled buds that day, unfurling as I write. All the purple and yellow irises were sold, and the many coloured daisies, the expensive stargazers were in fact the first to go. These stood high headed in my blue plastic bucket reserved for red roses. After I'd sold everything on the cart I was glad they were still there, because now I know I bought them for me. What was it they reminded me of, that wild brightness of an autumn sun, hurried yet warm?

Here in my slowly chilling living room
they've come alive, colouring my eyes again.
Reminding me of the longhaired one, his palms
like petals on fire. The man whose name I'll
never know. Yet it is part of some older memory,
coming to warm me in russet shades. Peeling
into the satin petals of roses I cannot grow here
in London. Transported in cardboard boxes
punched with holes from far off places I'll never
see India perhaps or Amsterdam. Their breath
catching the colours of those untraveled spaces
they left behind. Even if they were grown in
hothouse conditions closer to here, they still hold
that fine taste of orange sorbet on a Twi's Day in
another August some six hundred or more years
ago. While I sit here in the afterglow, loving
myself for continuing to believe in flowers and
colours when the rain is refusing to drench
anyone beyond a grey drizzle. Splintering others
thoughts and their dampest memories, while I
drink these orange rosebuds this August alone.

The Ghost kitten

Reading in the train was becoming a habit. It wasn't easy to manage the thick pages of a novel while balancing your briefcase on a slim shoulder strap and keeping your back firmly rested against the metal wall of the jumping compartment. But she was getting the hang of it and being able to enjoy the ride, and the read too. Never mind the fishwives squabbling and the young children with their basketfuls of glittering plastic clips with shrill voices and the blind man singing like there was no one else in the compartment. Enjoy the stark sound of thumping, as live bodies flung themselves onto the train as it pulled, slowing into the last station, making sure they got a seat all the way home, two hours away. Churchgate Station at peak time was a battlefield, living proof of Darwin's beliefs, she thought.

Sumita was finally beginning to adjust to the sounds of Bombay. It was only three months since she had arrived to work in her brother-in-laws friend's ad-firm. She wanted to be a filmmaker, someone who understood dreams. She had been reluctant to leave her father at first. But she was aching for a new life, anything different from the small town smells of fish frying in old oil and bells in the tiny temple room in Agartala.

Luckily she had found an interesting PG accommodation with an elderly Gujarati couple in a pleasant suburb of the city, not far from the sea. The tall gleaming white building, with new plants spilling in variegated shades off grilled balconies seemed the best bet in the street of slowly crumbling high rises.

'Only Gujaratis live here *beta*', Mrs. Mehta had proudly informed her. She would've guessed that anyway, even without looking at the names hooked up in the building lobby on little brass plates –there was a distinct smell of evaporating ghee and coriander paste with an unmistakable hint of *hing* in the air. Pungent, yet inviting. It reminded her of their neighbour in Agartala, Kanchan *mashi* who spent all her time making 'snakes'.

It had frightened her as a child to see tiny yellow squiggles sizzling in a black *kadai* and to be informed by the neatly clad lady next door that she was making 'snakes'.

She realized later that she meant snacks but pronounced it interestingly. She hadn't found it as funny as her father though. It was that familiar yet un-home smell that made her want to stay in Kshitij Apartments, 8th Road. It was close enough to walk to the station and it was a spotless new building as well, no crummy corners stinking of bright red dried *paan* stains.

The estate agents had made her do the rounds of the cheapest oldest buildings in every locality because she wanted to be able to walk to and from the station. She needed to save as much money as she could. Besides, walking Sumita believed was the best way to get to know a new city and its people.

The elderly couple were sufficiently friendly and fussing, but not too talkative. Luckily they had each other for company, and seemed content with that. Three days after she had moved in Mrs. Mehta, whose first name didn't seem to exist, almost giggled and confessed that after thirty-three years of marriage this was the first time her husband spoke to her like a person, almost like a friend. Sumita immediately missed her mother, on behalf of her father.

She watched the tiny woman, with round dimpled elbows and small rimless glasses take two cups of milky fragrant tea to the mini half-balcony where the couple watched the sun come up over the treetops. They spoke almost silently and crackled cream crackers between them, which they shared, dipped into the *masala* mixed tea.

It was a pleasant home to leave in the morning; she never felt like staying back, they seemed so complete by themselves. And it was an agreeable place to return to. She felt grateful for the simple hot meals her landlady provided and happy that the room she occupied had a separate entrance with its own corridor beside the kitchen. She had no patience for cooking. She watched Mrs. Mehta sometimes and quietly missed her mother. When she missed her too much she would leave the flat and go for a long walk, Bombay was relatively safe for a woman that way.

She loved the comfortable sound of the sea on old rocks. She would listen to her Walkman and hum, laying her other memories to sleep. But they were wakeful, those pictures of her home, her missing mother. No one knew where her mother had gone, one afternoon she had disappeared. Sumita had come home from college and her father had been sitting wide-eyed. 'She doesn't want to be found', he was holding a letter, which he refused to show her.

Sumita didn't want to believe him. She didn't understand the way he loved her mother. If he really did, why would she hear her crying out on the balcony almost every night? Her elder sister had died at childbirth, they had never been close she was much older, almost eleven years stood between them. But her brother-in-law Raman still kept in touch with them, he had remarried, a girl who was much younger but looked a lot like her dead sister. Sumita didn't visit him, but when he offered her a chance to leave Agartala by mentioning the ad-job she jumped at it.

Her father never showed Sumita her mother's last letter, he destroyed it he said 'I miss her too much'. She had been seventeen then, and she hadn't really believed her father. Why would her mother just leave? But somehow she had felt guilty and stayed. She knew he had a drink problem, though he was exceptionally discreet about it. Maybe she needed to meet someone who knew nothing and talk it over. It was over three years since her mother had gone. She remembered those late night blank calls at their house, had it been her trying to call Sumita?

She went out for a walk.

***

Dilip had been living with his brother and Radha, his brother's girlfriend for over eight months now. He wasn't happy with the arrangement. But it was the price he had to pay if he wanted to live in Bombay, which he did. This was the city for dreamers. He was a qualified Chartered Accountant; managing numbers that represented other people's hard earned money. He had to make sense of expenditure versus earning and it kept his mind jogging the thin line between bliss and boredom.

When Dilip wasn't calculating numbers or doing the rounds of the Income Tax officers file stacked desks he was dreaming.

Dilip wanted to be a pilot. He knew it was impossible. But that didn't stop him dreaming. Being alone in the evenings when he knew his brother and Radha wanted time alone in the little flat was the best time of his day. He went seeking the sea. Breathing the stink of dry fish and salt baked rocks shook his imagination awake and he was ten again, telling his father, 'When I grow up I want to be like Shiv Uncle, I want to fly a plane.'

Walking along the ocean's shore line was the closest he had come to soaring. It was too expensive and elite an occupation. He couldn't even console himself, postponing the possibility that some ten years later he'd have made enough money to educate himself and control the throttle of a wind-live bird, when all he had in his hand was an imaginary stick that had grown wispier over time.

Dilip walked for hours. Sometimes tracing dreams under his heels, pretending he hadn't made his CA exams, that there were other options open to him. He wasn't young. He didn't celebrate his birthday anymore and since no one in Bombay knew him they didn't ask, and his brother didn't have a memory for sentimental detail. He wondered how Radha stood for it. But then she seemed to enjoy the enslavement. Radha was an average cook, but she kept the two-room house spotless. Dilip slept in the living room, which had a small television and two chunky mattresses stacked to make a sofa, piled with mirror work spattered cushions. Radha loved green; everything in the house was a shade of leafy vegetables, and smelled as soggy. The walls in the flat were damp, which the monsoons made worse. The odd shaped corridor between the living room and kitchen served as a dining area for two, but they had to share a toilet.

Dilip was fanatical about saving money, the rent allowance he got wouldn't have got him a place for himself and it was better to live here than in a paying guest place where you had to share with strangers. Dilip didn't like meeting people much. This arrangement wasn't the best thing he could imagine, but his brother was familial enough not to expect any money from him towards the rent. He chipped in for the phone bill and bought the groceries twice a month. They shared a cordial un-intrusive relationship.

Dilip's brother, Dharam, was all male and loud voiced about his opinions. With Dilip however he was different. He liked to feel that his younger brother, despite having a job was dependent on him in some way. He believed in male bonding, that silent sharing which never really happened. He was as tall as Dilip and fairer, he hardly went out in the sun he spent all day at the Stock Exchange and the rest of the time he and Radha were either home or watching a Hindi movie. They loved Hindi movies. That's all they had in common.

Dilip didn't know how his brother had met Radha. He didn't know much about her other than that she was a primary school teacher with a paltry pay. Apparently her family didn't really care where she was. So his brother was unpressured in terms of tying the knot. Their own family didn't really care one way or the other. Dilip wasn't even sure if his parents knew about her. Once or twice when his mother had called Radha had answered the phone, and she had intentionally spoken in Hindi. Did she like being the maid equivalent? Dharam joked about it when they ate together sometimes. He didn't show her physical affection in Dilip's presence, which was a relief, but Dilip suspected he didn't show her much affection when they were alone either.

After a heavy meal, which was generally ordered in from the closest Punjabi Dhaba every Saturday, Dharam would smile, stretching his lips like a yawning animal and say, 'All my needs are met, what else does a man want!' He wouldn't even look at Radha but that was the closest she ever came to blushing. Dilip didn't understand them. They barely spoke to each other, Radha was too quiet, and she didn't joke. Maybe it was her dark framed glasses that kept her looking serious. He was never embarrassed in their midst, but he would escape the burden of making their company a crowd and walk outside their flat on Eighth Road.

He wondered if he ever had a girlfriend what their relationship would be like. But he wasn't likely to meet anyone, and anyway he wasn't looking. He was fine by himself. If he needed to talk about his dreams he went to the sea.

***

Eighth Road was a quiet, narrow and long road. It linked two main traffic choked roads but remained provincial. Magenta and white papery bougainvillea climbed wire meshed fences and fell over onto the tar blackness of the street. Neighbours walked dogs and rarely talked to each other while buying vegetables from the same vendor. Every morning at eleven he would holler in an almost animal tone, a sound everyone recognized as the call of the vegetable man but no one really knew what he said. No one asked. He brought fresh vegetables piled on a rickety wood and steel cart right to their doorstep, that's what mattered. The fresh splash of deep green curry leaves or paler curly edged coriander sprang like water on your sleepy face, that's what mattered.

There was an eccentric single woman who lived with three dogs in a tiny outhouse like structure, which she had made posh by erecting a bright yellow and white awning to shade her garden and her life from the peering neighbours. Sumita noticed her on many evenings sitting in denim shorts feeding her dogs biscuits and sipping from a large mug, tea maybe. She didn't seem like a coffee sort of person. Sumita had heard of this woman.

Rumour had it that she was the keep of a married Bollywood star; many men visited her at odd hours, so perhaps she was kept not by any one. She looked intelligent, but very alone. Sumita had been tempted to talk to her once when she was passing her bamboo fenced garden enclosure. She had heard from Mrs. Mehta, who had a friend in the Sindhi building. 'She's not a Sindhi, must be that's why she's like *that…*' Mrs. Mehta had left the word dangling like a half rotten tooth.

Sumita didn't believe all the gossipy innuendo about her being some loose woman. People, especially older married women without jobs were always suspicious about young independent women, who didn't apparently need a man. She had felt it at first when she had moved in with the Mehtas. Mrs Mehta had lost her gushy grin and become suddenly cooler than before when Sumita brought her male colleagues over one.

So she didn't bring any visitors over anymore, neither men nor women and tried to keep decent hours. She made it a habit to sleep at the Edit Suite if she had to stay on for an edit till four or five in the morning. She made up a cousin and said she was staying there. It was surprising that she could maintain her reputation of being a decent girl despite working in the infamous advertising world.

Mrs. Mehta didn't see anything wrong in Sumita staying over at her imaginary cousin's house. Mr. Mehta read his newspapers; he bought every single one and then went for a long walk with two of his friends. He was the sort of man who didn't share himself, not even when he smiled. It was as if he was smiling at some private joke.

They made an odd couple. Sumita wanted to get to know the single woman with her dogs, but dropping in on a stranger didn't seem all right in Bombay. In small towns you had a right to know what was happening in the neighbour's house. You could wander in and gossip over tea and crisp onion *bhajjia* fries. Sumita liked Bombay, but somewhere she began to understand that her loneliness would never really leave her. It had attached itself to her like a stubborn late afternoon shadow. It hadn't stayed behind locked in her room in Agartala.

***

Dilip was getting fed up with his sense of wandering. His walks were getting more and more predictable. He tried not to walk at the same time every day, because then he would bump into some familiar face. He would get home from work, shower, and change into his running shoes and jeans and nod to Radha and leave just before his brother arrived. Every week day he came home around 1am, knowing that they would have finished their dinner and watched television, their favourite quiz show hosted by their favourite Bollywood actor with his immense voice, and vinegar sharp humour. He had tried watching it with them, but his brother was too much of a show off with his insistent knowledge of useless trivia. He was the perfect quiz participant who had never yet entered a proper quiz.

On Saturdays afternoons he ate with them but left early so they had their flat to themselves and he had himself to himself. Dilip was walking down Eighth Road, imagining how beautiful this old bungalow would have looked in its time. His brother rented part of the top floor; the rest of the house was also let out to office going men who lived alone. Radha was the only female on the premises, that made his brother envied, which was just what he wanted.

The house was unkempt and peeling from the outer damp walls. An enormous over grown garden shielded the ground floor windows from the direct view of the street. It might have been a romantic place to live in.

Might have.

He should see if any of the other rooms were going cheap. Six months with his brother and living this kind of outdoor lifestyle per force wasn't suiting him anymore. He had come to a crossroads before he had expected to. He looked down the road. It was just past midnight. The lamplight was casting wavering silhouettes of live leaves onto the black road. It hadn't rained in a few days, but there was a rainy breeze picking up the fallen leaves, swirling them around in the empty gutter.

Dilip walked a few slow paces, wondering which way he should turn. Before he could take a step he heard a cat mewing. No it wasn't a cat; it sounded more like a kitten. He looked around. It seemed to coming from under a parked car. He bent down to take a look; there was no light under the car at all. The car itself looked like it hadn't been moved in a few years. It was a dirty blue Fiat, with dust collected on the edges of the windows in thick smears. Dilip heard the mew again it wasn't very loud this time. He knelt down and tried to look again.

'Can you see it?' A girl was standing beside him suddenly. He stood up in a hurry.

'Huh?' he said.

'The kitten, it's been crying for a while…I heard it last night as well' She was pretty in an unassuming kind of way. He was looking at her face lit by the falling yellow of the lamplight. Her hair looked unfurled, but curly, like she had hurriedly undone a plait, and her face was a little sleepy.

'Do you live here?' She had an interestingly distant sort of voice, like rain in thumping outside a corridor far from your room.

'You shouldn't be out so late…' Dilip said.

'Oh…I walk around this time every night. I live in that old bungalow'

She looked a taken aback.

'No no, it's not mine! But my brother rents a flat on the first floor. They've turned the bungalow into many individual flats.

The girl nodded, slowly smiling. It was a proper smile, he noticed, under the fluorescent light of the lamp post.

'I couldn't sleep' Dilip added.

She pulled her windcheater over her pajama top and smiled, 'We should look for the kitten…'

But they couldn't hear it anymore. Sumita tried calling to it, like her mother used to call to Billie, clucking her tongue against the roof of her mouth. But the kitten was gone.

And then they saw an old woman; she was hunched over a basket. She looked up at them and smiled. Her face was covered in fine wrinkles; it made her look more beautiful somehow. Her eyes were bright and she had a dark grey shawl pulled over her dirty white hair.

'Were you looking for the kitten? She's safe now. She escapes sometimes and I have to come and find her.'

The woman was sitting under the street lamp; they couldn't really see the basket because it was directly in her shadow. 'May I see it please?' asked Sumita craning over her shawl-covered shoulders. 'No…' she heard the old lady say.

Dilip and Sumita looked at each other both thinking the same thought, 'is she nuts'. When they looked up the woman with the basket wasn't there anymore. They hurried out into the darkness beyond the lamplight. She couldn't have walked away so fast. But there was no one on the long dark street except the two of them.

'Come let me leave you to your building,' said Dilip, 'it's late and it might rain'.

Sumita walked beside the dark unlit gutter wondering about ghosts.

They fell in step, together, under the yellow leafed lamplight.

Lions' Den

A mitav lit fire to the small heap of soggy labels. He had painstakingly torn them, each one of the five paper labels off the pint bottles, as he slowly glugged down the fluid fire. He had given up smoking that evening and it didn't seem to be working after seven hours of abstinence. He had to make it go away. He watched the smoky flame and the scattered black matches around the miniature bonfire. He was sitting by himself outside the bar that had finally been shuttered by the cops. It was 3 am. Rain clouds had collected in a thunderous cluster overhead.

Bombay-*ishtyle* monsoon, proper *filmi*. It would break soon. Proper obsessive, heavy raindrops, like a woman crying for a long gone lover.

Damned cops, but he was always nice to them. He had to be. He was going to be the pioneer of the Indian detective novel in English. He needed their input to build believable plots. Two and a half years at *The Times of India* as a staff reporter hadn't helped as much as he had hoped. The flame from the beer labels fell into a smokeless silence as the rain successfully fell. Every Saturday evening Amitav would find his way to the local beer joint and down a couple of pints at least and go through a pack of Four Squares if not two. He would watch people and imagine their lives outside this barely lit room with round stools and red cushions. Sometimes he'd imagine he had successfully chatted up some buxom female in a short skirt. He imagined all the girls he'd turned down at college, what were they doing now. He had waited instead for that sweet sixteen-year-old who would declare him her first and only love. No second hand goods for him; neither did he want just the rush of blood into unmapped places. He had wanted love. That had never happened and he had stupidly stayed a virgin.

'Fool', he had stubbed out his last cigarette last night and decided to quit. Both waiting and cigarettes. Maybe some woman would be drawn to a non-smoker. It seemed the way to get the girls these days. It had worked for Shyam. Raina and he were going home to her place every bloody night this last week. Her mother was out of town. Shyam was a closet smoker now, but man did he grin every morning and stroke his neck too casually when he was late into work. Shyam was a really sharp features writer.

Amitav had been nursing an ambition to be a 'real' writer, he read voraciously, and ate little. He was lean, and looked like a basketball player without the calf muscles. He led an intentionally isolated life, though he was popular at work and with his maternal cousins who he lived with. He had a tangy sense of humour, like his breath felt now after too many beers. He didn't feel so good.

It was the usual Saturday night gig, beers at Gokul and a kebab dinner at Bademiyyan's with the building gang. They always came back to Bade's after a few plates of stuffed *baida-roti* and chicken *tikkas* for the third and fourth round of beer and peanuts coated with thickened red *masala*.

But tonight he had a premonition of disaster.

He was hoping for a promotion from junior staff reporter; plus his piece on a socially relevant play was bound to be replaced by the news on the swanky naval Fleet Review. What a waste of energy and time, all those white-uniformed men parading, backs unnaturally straight. Shyam his senior had done that piece. It was good no doubt but so was his own piece, which was more current and relevant.

Amitav had read Shyam's second draft. It would definitely make the Sunday front page. He hated staff politics.

Shyam got bloody everything. Thank god they hadn't been here this evening. Shyam's ample triceps wound round Raina's neck, covering her deliciously low-cut *batik* shirt. But then they were possibly in better positions and barer. No more imagination leading into other people's beds. He decided to drink more than usual, besides he was missing the taste of nicotine under his tongue and the smell of it under his shirt.

The road was quieter now. The bar had emptied as easily as a bucket of rotten fish being poured back into the sea. Everyone had gone home after two huge Sardars had had a screaming brawl, which the cops had broken up. He didn't feel like going home. His sexy cousin Maya wouldn't be home till 5 am. It was maddening hearing her creeping home, breathless from hurried kissing in the dark tile-lined passageways. He wondered if she did more.

Maya had several good-looking guy friends. She had an awesome figure besides, so little wonder about the men. It was hard sleeping in the single bed four feet away from her curves making gentle slopes under the sheet. Even in the dark, under the patchwork lamplight that filtered into their room from the high-up ventilator, she was visible because he watched her.

Amitav would wait till she fell asleep; he'd listen for her breathing to fall into that even pattern then he'd watch her chest heave and fall. He knew he was being an idiot, but then her parents were just too liberal. They were both too old not to be able to tell that stains on his bed weren't spilt morning coffees. And that her nightshirt rising to her chin wasn't always a mistake. Maya loved teasing him. She often watched him rise from the bed and walk uncomfortably to the bathroom in the mornings, his body half turned away from her. He reminded himself every day, she's my sister.

She wouldn't be home yet, not so early on a Saturday night. Amitav stumbled to his feet and began to saunter home. His hair and shoulders began to drip with rain; a stream of water trickled down his shirt. The house was only a seven-minute walk away.

The stone and tar footpath stretched in a curved mile along the sea face. The pale yellow of the tall lampposts seemed paler through the sheets of water before his eyes. The massive structure of the gateway proclaiming architectural finesse to the Raj and its royalty lay oddly quiet. But then this sort of downpour wasn't romantic even to the most arduous gay couples. Amitav sniggered. No one was getting any under the domed archway and its dank shelter, smelling of acrid perspiration and pee. No, not tonight. That smell persisted even under the rain. He wasn't the only unlucky sod, he thought.

He was enjoying the trickling, caressing watery feel of this drunken walk home; he reached into his pants and felt the comforting warmth of the hair between his thighs. He sucked in the water that was pouring down his face in a deliberate slurp. He wanted to cuddle his *razai*; it's blue old silk against his bare face. He wanted to be dry.

Something creaked behind him in the rain he turned and saw that the Iron Gate, which barred the slope down to the jetty, had swung open. It was usually padlocked every evening. Maybe there was a couple risking the salt and spray of the Arabian Sea tonight after all. Amitav's voyeuristic urge swelled his mind and he felt suddenly awake. Ha, at least he'd watch some fun and then slip between the covers, happy. Let Maya come in after he was asleep for a change!

The jetty was thicker with rain and the flaring spray from angry waves. Everything was hissing like a hot pan dowsed with sudden water. The stones under Amitav's thick-soled shoes felt slimy, he caught hold of the cold iron bars of the gate for support and peered down the slope trying to catch sight of the couple he thought might be clasped against the shell and moss covered bastion. Would anyone risk being naked in this weather?

But there weren't any people braving the salt spray. It was silent except the rain and sea waves. A white lump of fabric lay unmoving a few feet away from him. Amitav was now truly awake and unaware of having drunk any beer at all. What was this weird thing? Some deep sea creature thrown up in the storm? Should he find out? Suddenly amorous humans seemed less interesting. He walked gingerly toward the white lump. It was glowing against the watery slope, a dull sort of glow. Amitav reached down and then stopped. He wasn't sure what it was.

It was horribly wet and dark, the Iron Gate creaked again, banging shut.

He shuddered.

Then suddenly civilization shook awake. A car whizzed by and someone screamed, 'Fuck man...life is beautiful...marry me tonight please, just for tonight...' The voice trailed off as the sound of the wheels swishing the street dimmed. A group of men hunched together were chortling over not being able to light a cigarette. They splashed by the gate and he could still hear their laughter on the breeze. The rain slowed. Amitav was still standing with the lump at his feet. Too small to be a person. He reached down and touched the soaked fabric. It wasn't cold, just very, very wet. He picked it up.

It was a beach bag, a girl's beach bag.

Amitav held it up against a street lamp and wondered. He'd take it to the cops tomorrow. Good excuse. He could easily ask questions and do some research for his detective plot. That's it; he'd walk into the Police Headquarters that was just round the corner from the Gateway and produce this suspicious bag. His mind was buzzing and he rushed home full of resolve. Amitav let himself into the house by the side entrance as quietly as he could. Maya's room was empty, good she wasn't back yet.

He began examining the contents of the soaked bag, they were wrapped in a thick duty free type clear plastic bag stuffed into the canvas outer bag. Sensible girl. He hesitated a second before opening the packet and examining what was wrapped inside a largish pink towel. Then his inquisitive instinct took over. He drew out the damp towel; some water had sunk through despite the plastic. He opened out the towel and laid it on his wide desk under the blue enamel lamp.

There was a pink and cream mass of clingy material in a wrung heap. He knew it must be a swimsuit, he dropped it to the floor. A pair of beige unworn lingerie lay under a paperback copy of Amitav Ghosh's *Glass Palace*. The underwear was attractive in a sensible sort of way. Half cotton and the other half lace covered. The edges of the book were curled with dampness. Interesting! Well read. Or maybe she had been trying to create an impression. There were also a couple of ball pens, one of which had leaked its sticky glue-like ink onto a corner of the pink towel in a green patch; clean comb, a brush with a few dark hairs in it. He examined the hair against the lamp, not very long. Two maroon hair clips, a half-finished pack of Juicy Fruit, a small pale pink satin toilet case, which he wasn't interested in. A paler pink silk scarf with brighter pink rosebuds embroidered along the edges. Very girly. Under the toilet case and scarf he noticed a thick leather covered journal.

There was no wallet. No identifying object.

He touched the cover of the journal; it felt dewy, not too damp. He felt inclined to shut the door and read. This might be interesting.

The pages inside the journal were slightly stuck, a few words here and there were smudged but it was overall dry and readable. There was no name on the flyleaf, just a sketch of a girl standing on a beach. Amitav turned a few pages, but the journal fell open to a page that was obviously often read. The handwriting was neat, not very small and not very curvaceous. What did this girl look like he wondered? He read.

'What lips my lips have kissed and where and why I have forgotten

...But summer sang in me a while that sings in me no more.'

He gave me that poem two days before he told me about the 'other' woman. Should I have opened the door last night when he dropped in? It was so late. How did he find me, no one he knows has this new address? Thank god the landlady and her daughter sleep so deeply. I'm glad I chose this flat with its separate entrance. Not that I've ever used it. He left me before I found this flat, before I got myself my own phone-line. But I know it's him that calls. I told Rakhee, she also feels it's got to be him, no one else uses that code, those two short rings…I know he still loves me…why does he come to see me if he doesn't. I left home for him. I told Maa I couldn't live my own life under her constant hawk-eye. She was unhappy, I know. She hasn't called for over three months. She must be really hurt. But I had to. I thought it might scare him into committing. It's been over five years now, and I'm not looking forward to my next birthday…how could I have guessed that all along there was this 'other' woman. She works with him apparently, same office, lives in the same building two floors below. They've known each other seven years…I guess I'm the other woman…I can't tell Maa she'll just say 'I told you, I warned you about flashy cars and their drivers…' Truth is she did, but my heart was telling me otherwise, so were his hands, his eyes, his lips, his…god when will I stop crying…'

Amitav almost wretched. Girls! Always crying over some jerk. Why couldn't they just give it back? How boring! The entry he had just read was dated early December. It was now July. A lot more pages were filled in, she obviously found comfort in spilling herself on paper...his head grew heavy and he realized it was almost 5am. He heard the front door creak open. Maya. He hurriedly dumped the diary into his top drawer and bundled the towel back into the wet bag, which he hid under his desk, behind the large wastepaper bin. Just then the room door opened. Damn, the swimsuit, he hurriedly kicked the swimsuit under the desk, and stood up.

Maya stood there her sequin and felt purse dangling from her bare arm. She was dripping wet. Her black silk blouse clung to her and her hair fell about her face like wet wool. She was obviously very high. She came close to him. He felt his own chest harden with hers. He could smell a familiar male smell rising from her wet hair.

'You're very tall Amit...' she slurred a little, he held her an arm's-length away from him. She allowed herself to be led to the bed. She lay down with her arms stretched above her wet head, and kicked off her heels. Her eyes closed. 'I feel so warm...we drank champagne, lots of pink bubbling stuff from tall glasses...not as tall as you...' she giggled then controlled herself. 'He's asked me to marry him...so I let him, he was very slow and I wasn't...hmm...' She had fallen asleep with her face on his hand.

Amitav felt self-conscious and responsible all of a sudden. He brought out her towel from their shared bathroom and threw it over her. He rubbed her down carefully, and then undressed her under the towel with unsteady hands. As much as he tried he couldn't avoid accidentally brushing parts of her skin. Her flesh was warm and sprinkled with goose bumps under his slow fingers. Once he had peeled off all her wet things he pulled a long nightshirt out from under her pillow where he knew she stuffed it every morning. He propped her against his taut shoulder and dropped the silken fabric over her head pulling it gently over the rest of her purring form, pulling the towel from her only when he had finally finished dressing her.

He was her elder cousin he repeated to himself, like an angry chant trying to ignore the rush of overwhelming warmth when his left hand had momentarily brushed fine curls while pulling off her tight suede pants.

Amitav went to bed thinking of women, but not of their bodies. His dreams of course were an untold story, a place where unexplored territory could be conquered and kept.

***

The next morning he awoke late and worked on his plot line, trying to incorporate the girl's bag into the story. Should his central character, the private detective, be a loud-mouthed Punjabi with an unerring eye for detail? Or, perhaps a Maharashtrian; silent and stoic with an appetite for buxom eastern women? It wasn't easy. He toyed with his idea all day. Apart from that it was an uneventful Sunday.

Maya was still sleeping when he went for a walk by the sea and watched yachts that he'd never sail in. Who owned these beautiful expensive creatures?

Amitav longed to light his customary cigarette and imagine himself among the rich and famous of Bombay, steering a splendid white yacht out of the bay towards the opposite coasts where most millionaires had their weekend retreats. His hand ventured to his shirt pocket, put it was empty. He felt cheated by himself.

When he got home Maya had showered and changed. She looked so different without her make-up. She was having tea with her parents and elder brother. He never joined their Sunday evening chats. He felt they should be entitled to their own family time and not be bothered by an orphan. They respected his reclusiveness.

He slept earlier than usual. He read.

He was re-reading his favourite Dick Francis, *Odds Against*, admiring the gritty characterization of Sid Haley. Maybe someday he would write like this. Stomach churning violence packaged in simple language. He must read more. Amitav heard Maya walking into the room. He hurriedly turned off his bedside lamp and turned his back to her side of the room. They were barely eight months apart in age.

He could smell her wonderful clean after shower smell of lime and talcum powder up against his face. 'I know you didn't touch me last night...I really respect you Amit. I'm glad it is dark...I couldn't have spoken otherwise...thanks I guess.' Her breast brushed his arm for the briefest instant and he longed to pull her toward him and hold her really tight. Just hold her. She was such a crazy girl. He heard her sliding down on her bed. He felt like she was waiting.

Was life always this crazy? Putting you into irrevocable situations? Amitav was annoyed at the sound of his thoughts. Love? God, he was beginning to sound like the lovelorn girl in the diary. He hadn't read the diary at all since last night. Maya had occupied his thoughts almost completely. He wondered now, what happened to the girl in the diary and her lover.

'I know you had company last night…' Maya was still waiting in the dark.

'What?' he sounded hoarse.

'The swimsuit' she replied plainly, 'interesting size…'

What should he tell her? He was unsure about going to the cops. Maybe someone had intentionally thrown the bag aside, getting rid of evidence and just forgotten the diary. No, that was just his own detective obsessed brain conjuring a plot where there was none. Maybe the girl had decided to get rid of every trace of the elusive man in her life. That was possibly it. He put his hand under his face, settling into the comfort of his own body. He had to sleep. The story would come to him if he plugged his brain. He had to ignore Maya it was the only way. Feign sleep and it would come.

He heard the door being bolted from the inside.

Suddenly the entire weight of Maya had settled on him. He stiffened. 'I want to…please I'll be married soon, then it'll be impossible…Amit you must know how I've been feeling…' He didn't say a word he didn't need to, he was crying. She didn't notice. After what sounded like an hour of silence he heard her breathe against his neck. Her hair fell over his face. She moved her slightly parted lips carefully over his eyes, barely breathing. He realized that somehow she had seen a lot of life; a lot more than he had realized. He let her twirl the ends of his hair and lie curled with her body soft against his.

**

He went to work wakeful after a night of no sleep. He noticed a crowd of people at the jetty. There were some policemen as well. He would normally have joined the pack to see what was happening. But his mind felt stretched. He hardly paid attention at work. He had to interview some workers who were protesting against a mill shut down. Drab. He sweated it out under a sky that was too blue after two days of the storm. He longed for the wetness of rain falling down his neck.

Maybe he should take Maya out for a coffee. Would she come to his bed again?

At lunch completing the crossword with practiced ease he came across a piece of news that startled him. He was turning the pages, irritable about how the crossword got so repetitive after a few weeks of relentless word finding. A tiny piece on the third page of the tabloid glared out so he read ahead:

'UNIDENTIFIED GIRL FOUND DEAD
A young girl aged between twenty and twenty-five was found dead near Gateway of India. The body was washed up in the early hours of yesterday morning. Police are still uncertain about the circumstances or cause of death. Foul play cannot be ruled out they said. The unidentified body has been sent for post-mortem. No one has come forward to claim the body. She was dressed in a white dress with no underclothing. The police declined to comment on it being a possible case of rape and murder.'

No underclothing. It stuck out.

Amitav felt the chill of the storm from the night when he found the bag. He left his lunch half finished. All the chicken biryani was over anyway and the veggie one was too dry. The canteen fellow was the one who didn't talk so he hadn't asked for any *raita* either. He went back to the third floor and asked his crime reporter colleagues if they had heard anything about this unidentified girl.

'So many chicks disappear in this city Amit…no we're not covering the story. I think Vineeta knows someone at *the Mid-day*…trust them to spice things up with a suggestion of rape and murder! Tabloids, huh?'

Amitav had drawn a blank after that because Vineeta was out of town. He wasn't even sure what exactly to ask. He'd have to go back and read the diary. He couldn't wait till he clocked out. He filed his hurried piece on the mill and why it was an icon of Indian industry. He almost ran all the way to his desk in Maya's room. She was not there, so he could concentrate.

The girl's diary lay there, forgotten, silent among his story ideas. He opened it again, interested now. He flicked through to the end. These latter pages would hold some clue maybe.

May 29th
The call came today. He wants me to write for him. I can't believe it. I've been struggling so long, now finally a real offer! What if I blow it!? Tomorrow at 3 I've to meet him for coffee to discuss the details. I don't know what to wear. I must appear completely

professional. Women never get taken seriously
otherwise!

Did women only think of men and
clothes? But then men thought of little else apart
from women and their clothes. He flipped the
page...an undated entry.

Someone was calling my number frantically
all afternoon. There have been several bleeped
messages on the answering machine. But no words.
So like him. Anyway, I'm going to concentrate on
work now. The meeting was a success. I've spoken to
Rakhee and put together a proposal as well. These
business tycoons can be monsters if you aren't careful
she said. I have such little knowledge of their world.
She's been seeing Rakesh for seven and a half years
and his wife still doesn't know...I guess that's what
she meant...they're weird. I don't get a pleasant vibe
from this man. He's older than what my father would
be. So I guess he's safe! He told him so. He said
something peculiar... 'I'm not your father young lady

and don't intend to be' Something like that…it made
me uncomfortable. But it is work and he's committed
to a hefty sum. This might be the break I've been
waiting for. What a stroke of luck meeting him at
Rakesh's last dinner party. He isn't ashamed to stroke
Rakhee's knee under the table or her face in front of
his wife. How come she's so blind…maybe she just
wants to ignore it, pretend. Don't we all…damn
women can be so silly so self-defeating! If, only…if.

Then it went on for a bit again about love
and some soppy stuff about her guy. Amitav
tried not to allow it to irritate him. He flipped
forward to another page. This entry seemed
hurriedly written. The words a mere scrawl. It
was dated last Thursday.

He's invited me to a yacht party on Saturday.
He says he wants me to meet his friends so I can
gauge and understand his character etc. from up
close. He says he thinks it might be an interesting
exercise to write up the experience to show him proof
of my work. I guess it's a good idea. I'm going to wear

Orange cat and others

my pink pearls. They'll go beautifully on the pale shell pink scarf with the roses and my cream dress. I'm not going to take my swimsuit though he insisted that I should. It has been hot and well maybe there's no harm…and the wives will be there I guess, sipping wine and chatting about nothing. They only read Shobha De…maybe it'll be fine! My swimsuit is pink and cream too, I guess I can't be too careful. But I must dress right. I'll take the sun hat Mandy presented me when she came from Spain…My life is just about to start…I know it is…

Amitav felt sick. How would he know? The pink and cream swimsuit? He couldn't be sure who this girl was…was the bag linked to the dead girl? He read on.

How, how could I be so stupid?????????

There are four men here, and I'm the only female thing for miles in sight. We're at some weird film set type of cottage in the hills that surround Mandva beach. I can't even see the beach. There's a pool here it's deliciously blue and I like an idiot wore

343   *anwesha arya*

my swimsuit under my dress I'm dying to plunge
into the water and drive this heat out of my
head...but I won't. They were trying to get me to
drink...I made some religious excuse...OH GOD!
There's a cane bed laid out beside the pool under a
shelter of some sort...it's all like the setting for some
B-grade film in which I seem to be acting
inadvertently...I'm pretending to write some notes.
I'm sitting in a hammock under a grove of mango
trees. It's hot even in the shade...maybe it's my
mind!!! I got such a shock when I arrived all dressed
up and then I see these men, all except him, in office
clothes...One of the guys he's huge and darker than
anyone I've ever seen before! His nose is so
unpleasant like a piece of rat eaten toffee...yeugch it
is gross he's actually wearing a full three-piece suit.
The other two are in nylon shirts, which are
pretending to be silk! They've got a cricket game
going on so I decided to act like one of the guys...they
didn't expect a girl dressed in pearls and dainty shoes
to be one of the guys and know all about cricket. It's

the only way of fending them off for a bit I guess...I can't tell if I'm scared or just repulsed and shocked at myself for not realizing.

Amitav began wishing that this wasn't a journal written by a real person. But he knew it wasn't that simple. His protective instinct was wide eyed again. He turned to the next entry it was marked as few hours later.

When we came into the house I was actually terrified. There are only two men servants on these premises...no one else. I wish I could tell them I know someone who owns one of these posh beach resort type houses here...The house is hideously done up...all velvet and dark furniture and odd looking paintings of headless animals and faceless women. Eerie and sick. When I stopped writing earlier I could hear him asking his friends which swimsuit he should wear...I wonder if he's ever seen himself in the mirror. He's all middle, what swimsuit would hold that stomach! A Russian one maybe! How easy it is to find things funny when you're scared sick. Then I heard him

actually say 'how should I get her, tell me...come on
*tell me, just **help me***'.

And one of the other guys said, 'Just jump on
her while she's reading in the hammock'. They
obviously didn't realize I could hear them. I didn't
dare turn to face them, let them think I was reading
not writing. I wish Amitav would save me...

He sat up. Amitav, me? What the...?!
Then he realized she'd written how she had been
reading Amitav Ghosh's novel...still, how
weird! He began to feel helpless, but he had to
read, just another page anyway.

I can't bear to think of Burmese royalty...all rich
people are sick. Is it the money...do they really think
they can buy anything? I'm not for sale. No way.
And I won't be robbed either! NO WAY! They're all
sitting to lunch. I pretended I'm fasting. So fucking
lame. But they bought it. I wonder if they believe in
God...I doubt it. It was so repulsive the way he was
obviously trying to impress me with his wealth.
Yacht indeed, we came across in a speedboat with just

enough room for the two sailors from the Club and the five of us. I asked where the others were and they pretended like everyone had pulled out last minute! And I was born yesterday! Actually I feel like I was... He asked me if I wanted to leave if I was uncomfortable. I said I trusted him and as long as he said I had no reason to worry I'd be okay. Reverse psychology works sometimes, but only when skin is not buffalo thick! I feel like a wobbly jelly-baby. When his rat-eaten nose friend whipped out a pistol I had to stare up into the sun to feel strong. I suddenly realized. If they were to dump my body here somewhere no one would even know I was missing. Rakhee and Rakesh have gone for the long weekend to Shirdi and god knows where else. They haven't taken their mobiles because of his wife and other valid reasons. I should own one, but I can't afford one...I was dreaming of getting one once this biography was published...biography my ass. He was standing in chest high blue water ordering the servant to serve him his scotch on the rocks and to place two beer bottles on a tree a few feet away from the poolside. He actually aimed and shattered both. IMPRESSED! YUCK!!!!

Later: *I went looking for the loo. Imagine my state when I see the toilet door is made of frosted glass. I didn't even pull down my swimsuit. I just held it aside and let go! What a place. I've walked into the lion's den, as they would say in a spaghetti western. I truly have. One of the men palled up to me after lunch. So I began describing them as caricatures saying I'd write a story about them! I called him a spoilt Greek Tycoon like Jackie Onassis' husband...whatshisname... Albatross, no... Aristotle! Ha, and the two goons are Hindi film villains I said...and the rat eaten face was a Mafioso Sicilian style. Then I said how I felt that it was like walking into the Lion's Den. And he said 'yes...and it's amazing to escape the lion's den without a single scratch'. It sounded almost ominous. Anyway, we're leaving now. One of them has got a call and has to get back to shore...so we're leaving. Thank God!*

That was the last entry in the half-filled journal. Amitav laid it shut on his desk. There was nothing to do but wait for the next report once the post mortem results were released. It could take a few days before the police released that information. He felt uncomfortable but he didn't know what to do. Should he tell Maya? Maybe she would understand. He heard her giggling on the phone, obviously to some guy and decided against it. He sat very still, with a pen in his hand.

***

A week later Amitav was scanning the afternoon papers for news. On the fifth page in a tiny side column he read a few lines:

DEATH BY DROWNING

Mumbai Staff Reporter

The post-mortem on the unidentified young woman found near the Gateway of India last week after the cyclonic storm revealed that the death was caused by drowning. There is no more any suspicion of foul play. There wasn't a single scratch on the body.

Amitav read the last line again.

Orange cat and others   ~2020~

Anwesha Arya, a poet, author and academic, is happiest when she is reading, with her cat Pasha Alexandrina nearby. She has previously published book chapters on Indian film, linguistics. Her poetry and analysis have appeared in several literary and academic journals. Photography and poetry, law making and ancient ideas are her constant companions.

She lives and writes in a tiny thousand-year-old town in Southeast England. Her actor husband, four fantastic children, cat and five friendly fish maker her house a home.

<u>Cover photo credit:</u>

'Daisy in the blue'
by Anwesha Arya

Back cover photo
Fairy lights in the afternoon sun

[Author's private collection: Arya Assets]

Author Photo: Sanaaya Zarina Arya

Printed in Poland
by Amazon Fulfillment
Poland Sp. z o.o., Wrocław

60710744R10209